"Thank you for this book. We desperately need safe churches, but women can't create them on their own. We need men to listen, humble themselves, and change—just like Andrew has done in these pages as he has elevated women's voices. This book will haunt you—and it should. It is the right book at the right time. Don't just read it. Feel it. Grieve it. And then go and do something about it."

Sheila Wray Gregoire, author of *The Great Sex Rescue* and founder of Bare Marriage

"Gender is a war zone, today and ever since Adam and Eve passed from Eden into the realm of lust and anger. There is a cost to being a man, but the violence women have endured, emotionally, physically, and sexually, let alone overt and covert misogynistic cultural norms, makes the cost of being a woman vastly more difficult. And nowhere is this truer than in most churches. Andrew Bauman has with immense wisdom and humility addressed the exegetical, theological, cultural, and traumatic bonds that need to be broken to create not only equity and safety but flourishing for both men and women. This book is a tour de force for more honest and holy conversation and transformation."

Dan B. Allender, PhD, professor of counseling psychology and founding president of The Seattle School of Theology and Psychology

"Andrew Bauman goes beyond the obvious that the church has not been safe for victims of abuse. In this book he gathers together a chorus of women who love Jesus yet sing the same sad song. Striving for purpose and place in God's church, yet finding themselves dismissed, devalued, and at times degraded because they are female. We must do better."

Leslie Vernick, MSW, relationship coach, international speaker, and author of seven books including the bestselling *The Emotionally Destructive Marriage*

T0349906

"Is your church failing the women in it? Is it a safe place to belong? Is everyone able to show up and participate as their full selves? What if your women are compromising their own voices and contributions, making themselves smaller to serve faulty theology and the insecurities of the male leaders? What if you don't see it? Are you unintentionally harming people in your church? Are you willing to learn how this might be so? Dr. Andrew Bauman resources the voices of women—like the ones you minister to—helping others collaborate in experiencing the fullness of Christ for his people. May more men and women in the church model his humility and bravery!"

Aimee Byrd, author of *The Hope in Our Scars* and *Recovering from Biblical Manhood and Womanhood*

"Dr. Andrew Bauman has done the difficult and courageous work of researching women's experiences within the church. The findings are heartbreaking and reveal the extent to which the church is often a context for the significant and subtle harm of women. This is a critical inflection point for the Christian community, and if we are willing to listen, *Safe Church* can lead us into much greater honesty, grief, and renewal. *Safe Church* is sure to offer valuable insights to pastors, church leaders, and members, but it is the way Andrew listens, honors, and elevates the voices of women that we have the most to learn from."

Jay Stringer, psychotherapist and author of *Desire* and *Unwanted*

"Bauman goes to great lengths to address abusive behavior in the church and behind closed doors in *Safe Church*. Weaving his own journey into the work, he unearths weighty issues alongside his readers. He's never preachy but offers a holy imagination of what could be. With humility, he invites us to reckon with faulty theology and live into safe and grace-filled spaces."

Tiffany Bluhm, author of *Prey Tell*

"Thank you, Andrew, for making this topic of a safe church (for women and girls) so important to you that you would expend years, energy, and personal resources to listen to thousands of women reflect on their experiences, grapple with your own story vulnerably, and engage others so honestly that you get hate mail. You call us to painful memories, healing narratives, broken silences, and honoring relationships. Weaving research, stories, and theology together, you guide us to live mind, body, and soul in safer ways so that we might practically cocreate safer churches and ministries."

Dr. Nancy Murphy, executive director emeritus,
Northwest Family Life Learning & Counseling Center

"*Safe Church* is a shining example of personal and institutional accountability. Dr. Bauman unflinchingly takes on the history of sexism in the church and its perpetuation in many modern-day Christian organizations by giving credence to victims' stories as well as hard data. By breaking down both overt and subtle examples of sexism and misogyny in the church, he holds up a mirror to deeply ingrained behaviors, practices, and beliefs."

Tiffany Yecke Brooks, PhD, author of
Gaslighted by God and *Holy Ghosted*

SAFE
CHURCH

HOW TO GUARD AGAINST
SEXISM AND ABUSE
IN CHRISTIAN COMMUNITIES

DR. ANDREW J. BAUMAN

BakerBooks
a division of Baker Publishing Group
BakerBooks.com

© 2025 by Andrew J. Bauman

Published by Baker Books
a division of Baker Publishing Group
Grand Rapids, Michigan
BakerBooks.com

Printed in the United States of America

Library of Congress Cataloging-in-Publication Data
Names: Bauman, Andrew J., author.
Title: Safe church : how to guard against sexism and abuse in Christian
  communities / Dr. Andrew J. Bauman.
Description: Grand Rapids, Michigan : Baker Books, a division of Baker Publishing
  Group, 2025. | Includes bibliographical references.
Identifiers: LCCN 2024005420 | ISBN 9781540903976 (paper) | ISBN 9781540904485
  (casebound) | ISBN 9781493446995 (ebook)
Subjects: LCSH: Women in Christianity. | Women—Religious aspects—Christianity.
  | Sex discrimination against women—Prevention. | Psychological abuse—
  Religious aspects—Christianity.
Classification: LCC BV639 .B38 2024 | DDC 248.8/43—dc23/eng/20240327
LC record available at https://lccn.loc.gov/2024005420

Some names and details have been changed to protect the privacy of the individuals involved.

Cover design by Laura Powell

The author is represented by WordServe Literary Group, www.wordserveliterary.com.

Baker Publishing Group publications use paper produced from sustainable forestry practices and postconsumer waste whenever possible.

25 26 27 28 29 30 31   7 6 5 4 3 2 1

To my mom.
A woman who suffered so deeply
yet never lost hope in the goodness of God
and the power of Christian community.

CONTENTS

INTRODUCTION

We must never agree to "protect" the name of God by covering ungodliness. In Ephesians 5:11, Paul warns us not to participate in the deeds of darkness but instead to expose them.

Diane Langberg, *Redeeming Power*

It has taken every last inch of Christy's heart to keep believing in a God who is *for her*. She felt called to ministry from a young age, but Christian school teachers and pastor after pastor instructed her that her gender prohibited her from teaching the gospel, especially from the pulpit. Still, the passion to serve stayed with her, and after college she went to work in full-time ministry. She only made minimum wage, but this ministry also helped cover tuition if a staff member wanted to continue on to seminary, and Christy wanted to teach and preach the gospel.

Her boss quickly shut that dream down. They would not support that but encouraged her to "consider a counseling degree instead." So Christy settled and decided to pursue a master's degree in counseling and forgo her dreams of being a pastor.

This led her to the ministry-approved seminary where she was exposed to a good ole boys' club that would deeply mark her.

She often felt uncomfortable due to a male professor's continued sexual innuendos during Christy's group supervision classes, but when he showed her a video with sexual undertones during their one-on-one supervision, she'd had enough. Christy went to the only female professor on staff and told her what happened. That female professor was fired the next day. Even worse, eight other female students said that this male professor had been inappropriate with them as well, but when they threatened to take him to court, they were told they would not graduate if they pursued legal action.

While Christy was never physically touched at seminary, the sexism and abuse she experienced scorched her spirit in immeasurable ways, and those scars still remain.

Christy is my wife, which is perhaps why her story of harm has been the loudest for me. It is, sadly, not unique in any other way. In my therapy office, I have heard hundreds of similar stories of women receiving harm from Protestant churches and parachurch ministries. Christy's story is just one of thousands of stories in which a Christian community refused to offer safety to women and, worse yet, gaslit and silenced those who had been harmed and mishandled.

We in the church, especially leaders, must learn to listen to women's experiences and learn to be better allies to women. But where do we begin? What is the problem, and how big is it, really? Finding these answers is why I took on this project and have spent three years gathering data and listening to thousands of heart-breaking stories from women in the church. These women want the church to change. They love the church and desperately want to be conduits of healing transformation to assist in fostering safety and equality for all within Christian community. In sharing their stories with me, they have given me a great gift, and in writing this book, I attempt to honor the gift that has been given to me. Together, I hope we can not only name the problem but also create practical steps toward real change, reclamation, and healing.

What Is the Problem?

If the past few years have taught us anything, it's that the church has failed women. From sexual abuse scandals involving high-profile pastors and ministry leaders, to the exposure of the decades-long systemic cover-up of sexual harassment and mistreatment of women in the Southern Baptist Convention, to harmful theology that has chased women from the church to find community and safety elsewhere, it's evident that something is clearly broken. Women do not feel safe in church.

We must change not for God's sake but for our own—the sake of women and men and the church. Christians represent God as protector and liberator, not oppressor. As a reader, you may have a somewhat different perspective than I do, but I hope you can remain open, understanding, and compassionate as you hear these women's stories and come alongside me as we explore this issue in greater depth so that, together, we can help women feel safer in church.

Where This Book Began

I was a pastor before I became a therapist, and little did I know then how much my church experience would inform my work for the rest of my life. I got my undergraduate degree in Bible and religion, and I didn't really think of another career path beyond full-time ministry until I began working as a youth and college pastor.

During my time in ministry, I learned a lot. I saw the glory and mess of church. I experienced the beauty of feeling God's presence and the heartbreaking sear of my own and others' betrayals. I enjoyed most of what I did, but something was missing. I didn't feel that I could truly be myself or that I fit into the church culture. After a year or so, it became clear to me that my calling was more about speaking truth into church leadership systems than being a part of church leadership. This began my journey into graduate school, where I studied to be a psychotherapist.

I couldn't leave my theological roots behind, and I wanted to integrate them into my work as a therapist, so I chose to study at the Seattle School of Theology & Psychology. This school opened my eyes to trauma and abuse in my own life, in the lives of those around me, and in institutions—including the church. I began to see how unchecked systems could negatively impact the marginalized and the underrepresented. I became a sponge. After graduating and writing a few books, I founded the Christian Counseling Center: For Sexual Health & Trauma.

At first, I wanted to focus my efforts on helping men heal from deceptive sexual behaviors and patterns of abuse. But soon after, I also became a full-time advocate for women who had suffered due to these male attitudes and behaviors. I admit that some of those damaging attitudes were mine too. I needed God's radical kindness to show up and show me the truth. Through his loving shattering and healing, I have experienced years of painful maturation and increased self-awareness that led to greater humility (and lots of therapy) and to my passion for this topic of "safe church."

Women Will Show the Way

Women pioneers of the faith have never gotten much press. Not wanting women to share a seat at the table, many men in church leadership have not taken a posture of self-reflection and humility but rather of defensiveness and reactivity. And sadly, many good, Bible-believing Christians think that's what the Bible demands and that it is God's ordained order. It's not, despite what you may have been taught. When we silence women, we silence part of God and what God wants to teach us. God has much bigger plans for us all and for how we live within our churches and on this earth, but it's our responsibility to do the work to turn those plans into reality.

The purpose of the qualitative study that led to this book was to understand the presence of sexism and abuse in the Protestant church. To that end, I first connected with over twenty-eight hundred women with professional or volunteer experience in the Protestant church who agreed to complete a questionnaire about their experience. The second part of my study included in-depth interviews with eight of my survey respondents about their experiences while working or volunteering in their church.[1] These eight stories, as well as written responses from many other women who participated in the study, will be highlighted throughout this book.

This book is my attempt to elevate the voices and stories of women who have been silenced within Christian communities, many of whom have been deeply harmed, abused, neglected, and disregarded within the churches where they worked, volunteered, and in many ways dedicated their entire lives to serving. One of the many discoveries from my questionnaire was that *82 percent of respondents agreed that sexism plays a role in the church*. Let that sink in for a minute.

It's time for us to take action to make the church a safer place. And to be clear, the burden of this work falls to *men*, not women. In the United States, 87.1 percent of pastoral positions are held by men. Men must lead this transition if we are to see real and lasting change within the church.[2] Men in positions of influence, leadership, or inherent power by nature of their gender need to listen to women who have been on the front lines of Christian ministry and learn from them. This is the only way we can invoke change in the church and create safer places of worship for all.

A Road Map and an Invitation to Readers

Here is a quick overview of our journey ahead. In chapter 1, we'll look at the problem of sexism and abuse in the Protestant church and how it is disproportionately impacting women and also hurting men. In chapter 2, we'll consider why it's important to listen to women and learn from their experience within the church. In chapter 3, we'll discuss the historical experience of women in the church; in chapter 4, we'll look at Jesus's relationship with women. Then we will address problematic biblical passages that have been used as weapons against the vulnerable in chapter 5 and problematic theologies and teachings in chapter 6. We will dive into the complexity of trauma and abuse in chapter 7 and consider the church's present-day engagement with women in chapter 8. In chapter 9, we will discuss how men can begin to be the change we want to see in a safe church. In chapters 10 and 11, we'll discuss how we can start healing the wounds and look at concrete steps we can take toward creating safe churches. A word of caution: reading these pages and hearing these women's stories will be difficult.

For Men

Men, looking deeply into yourself and your own sexist, abusive behaviors and toxic belief systems will be incredibly challenging and somewhat daunting. It may feel like putting a frozen hand in warm water: it will hurt like hell at first, but over time, the pain will release and give way to the much-needed thawing so your hand can function again. It will be tempting to hear some of these stories and excuse yourself. But you don't have to be an overt sexist to be part of the problem. Men have been socialized since they were very young to believe that, on some level, women are less than— and the other guys have the problem, not us. Author and activist Tony Porter, in his powerful TED Talk, says,

> Collectively, we as men are taught to have less value in women, to view them as property and the objects of men. . . . You see, we have to come to understand that less value, property, and objectification is the foundation and the violence can't happen without it. So, we're very much a part of the solution as well as the problem.[3]

As men, we must own our misogyny and our violence toward women and begin to change the heartbreaking, all-too-common narrative. Silence is not okay! This is a man's issue, and we must first address the violence within ourselves before we can fix what is broken elsewhere.

Sadly, those who have been most harmed and impacted by sexism and abuse are normally the only ones who have had the courage to speak out against it. Victims have borne the burden of speaking up. Men have had the privilege of being ignorant to our own abuses against women, as we have been living in what Porter calls the "man box," or society's unconscious blessing of misogyny. For years, women have been leading us and teaching us how to address our own violence, and many courageous women I know are tired of fighting a man's battle for them. Those of us with male privilege and power must pick up what moral indignation we left behind long ago and stand up to other men when this sad cultural norm comes bursting into our lives.

Men are at a crossroads. We must take ownership of our own violence against women and against each other. Those of us who are church and ministry leaders can begin the process of creating a safe church with *ourselves*. Men who have not addressed their own issues of violence and abuse will surely continue them, even unintentionally. Tragically, throughout history, the bad behavior of men in power has been more the norm than the exception, and while most men today may not be actively sexually harassing or assaulting women, we enable this behavior through ignorance and silence even in our most sacred places—our churches. Turning the tide in intimate relationships from one of power and control over others to one of equality and mutual respect will take all of us.

One of the ways we can start doing this is by beginning the process of listening to women's experiences in the church.

For Women

Women, reading this book may bring up very painful memories you may have tried to forget. Don't run from them but toward them. Tend to your sensitive, wounded places when you get too close. The weight of being a woman in this world is a heavy burden to bear and can many times be a lonely and desperate place. You will hear from other women who know what you are feeling. Just know that you are not alone.

Many of you have known these painful stories deep in your body. Some of you have not known how to process the trauma you have experienced; others of you have grieved, mourned, and healed from your church pain. Regardless of where you are in your journey of healing, my hope is that this book deepens your faith and your heart for the church. That may sound counterintuitive for a book that is calling out abusive patterns in the church, but I argue that we cannot taste the goodness of the resurrection until we have the courage to sit in the pain of the crucifixion. A deeper understanding of sexism and abuse in the church can be a part of that much-needed death so that we as a church can move into the fullness of life. I invite you to feel the pain in the pages ahead and to grieve, wail, curse—whatever you need to do to uncover the deep hope that we as the people of God can bring heaven to earth.

ONE

So, What Exactly Is the Problem?

Imagine if every church became a place where everyone is safe, but no one is comfortable. Imagine if every church became a place where we told one another the truth. We might just create sanctuary.

Rachel Held Evans, *Searching for Sunday*

When I was a youth and college pastor nearly two decades ago, I served in several churches with all-male leadership structures. At the time, this was comfortable. These people looked like me, thought like me, spoke like me, and had similar views about God, church, and gender roles. My parents and the church I was raised in had instilled these views in me from an early age, and I took them with me into my adult years and the ministries I led.

In my childhood church, there were many unstated norms men and women were to follow to be in "good standing." Church men were supposed to treat women with respect in their presence, but when women were not present, men were often dismissive and judgmental about them. This banter about women was acceptable and often labeled "guy talk" in an effort to assuage any guilt for how rude it actually was.

The culture was remarkably similar when I entered the ministry. Many men in leadership positions were dismissive of women, acted superior, and believed male leadership roles were divinely appointed. Women's voices were not only discouraged but often even considered irrelevant to the important work of God. Women were only there to complement our essential calling and mission. Complementarian viewpoints (which involve a gender hierarchy that subordinates women to men) and patriarchy were ingrained in the gospel as I understood it. I was unaware that God views both genders as equal. I didn't realize that the way I viewed women wasn't honoring to God and that the church system was oppressing them.

What I Wish I'd Understood Then

While this book focuses on women's experiences in the church, we should first establish this conversation in the context of our history and culture. In the United States, women have historically faced unique gender-related challenges. Even now, in some sectors, women still have to fight for the same rights that have always been afforded to men, particularly regarding salary scale and career advancement opportunities.[1] Moreover, those in positions of power with the ability to either uphold or create societal norms and laws are often males who continue to support themselves and their interests. This is largely unconscious—though, in some circumstances, men certainly do consciously choose to jealously cling to power. But conscious or not, women in many fields suffer from chronic underrepresentation and are fighting to have their voices heard and to gain a seat at the table.

In nearly all industries, women face significant challenges unique to their gender. Consider the landmark 2015 Elephant in the Valley study, which examined the experiences of women in the technology industry. The findings indicated that 84 percent of the women had been told that they were too aggressive.[2] However, many women stated that they did not want to be seen as either too weak or too aggressive and found themselves trying to walk this difficult tightrope, an invisible burden that most men have the privilege of never having to consider.

One of the most concerning findings from the Elephant in the Valley study was the fact that 60 percent of women reported unwanted sexual advances, and of those who reported them, 60 percent were dissatisfied with the outcome of their reporting.[3] These women's experiences are far from uncommon; women face unwanted advances, mistreatment, and even abuse in nearly every industry and sector of society—but most particularly in male-driven fields where gender inequalities are pervasive.

This brings us to the field of Christian ministry. For the purposes of this book, *Christian ministry* is defined as serving in either paid or unpaid positions in a local church body. Christian ministry has been one of the most historically male-driven fields in America, even though women make up 61 percent of Americans attending religious organizations.[4] Only 14 percent of congregations in America are led by women, according to the National Congregations Study.[5] Though, as noted, women face oppression in a variety of sectors, this oppression is particularly prevalent in the Protestant church. In 2017, the Barna Group found that 77 percent of Americans were comfortable with there being more women than men in the workforce, yet only 52 percent of evangelicals were comfortable with it. Evangelical Christians were likewise the most hesitant group in Barna's study to accept women as leaders. When asked whether they were comfortable with a woman as CEO, only 77 percent of evangelicals responded yes as compared to 94 percent of Americans as a whole.[6]

The Barna study also stated that these responses may be attributed to the more traditional views on women's roles in the home and in child-rearing that are commonly espoused by evangelicals.

This is unsurprising, given that a fundamental, literalist reading of the Bible, which is embraced by many conservative Christian traditions, interprets women as being in a subordinate position to men. Still, it is striking to see data that suggests a vast majority of evangelicals and men in leadership positions have such an overall negative view of women in key leadership positions.

And this leads us to many of the foundational problems we see in the church today in regard to how so many women feel alone, underrepresented, and fundamentally unsafe in church experiences. Women haven't felt seen as equals. They have felt torn between what they experience as God-given callings to lead and man-given orders forbidding them to lead, resulting in disorientation and spiritual confusion. Also, due to this lack of female representation in leadership, men often doubt women's capabilities and do not give them a safe place to talk about their differing experiences.

Fortunately, in the wake of the recent #ChurchToo movement and the numerous accounts of pastors exposed in scandals, the conversations around power, abuse, and women's roles have been evolving in the church. These conversations have led me to consider a series of questions about the church and its current leadership structures, and what meaningful changes the answers to these questions could lead to.

How have certain theological interpretations impacted women's experiences in the church?

In what ways have traditional male leadership roles impacted women?

We are familiar with the headline-grabbing stories of pastors who have been driven from the church in the wake of sexual abuse and scandal, but what about the experiences of women every day in our churches and pews?

How do sexism and misogyny play out in the lives of women who have experienced them?

I wish I'd asked these questions years ago, but I'm glad I finally have. I hope the answers I've found can help other church leaders create safer, more affirming spaces for women. If we listen to women who have lived negative church experiences, we can learn how to create churches and places of worship of equality.

Establishing a Common Language

Before we talk about how we can guard against sexism and abuse in church communities, we first need to define them. Even the words *sexism* and *abuse* can make people uncomfortable. Additionally, sexism is often viewed as a political term; it's important we first strip away our political bias and personal defensiveness before we examine these terms.

Defining Sexism

A basic definition of *sexism* is "prejudice or discrimination based on sex."[7] *Prejudice* is a preconceived notion of who someone is without having much data about who they actually are. *Discrimination* is treating someone unjustly because of a perceived difference from you. Professors and psychologists Dr. Peter Glick and Dr. Susan Fiske divide sexism into three categories: hostile, benevolent, and ambivalent.[8]

Hostile sexism is defined as "beliefs and behaviors that are openly hostile toward a group of people based on their sex or gender"—such as misogyny, the hatred of women.[9] *Misogyny* can also be defined as a contempt and/or prejudice against women. It is possible for a person to hold misogynistic beliefs while still caring about the welfare of women. Many people, male and female, hold sexist beliefs without even fully realizing what they are or how they impact the world around them.

In general, most churches do not seem to fall under this category of outright and open hostility toward women, although, of course, there are some outliers. Consider the misogynistic comments of

23

Pastor Stewart-Allen Clark from First General Baptist Church in Malden, Missouri, in a 2021 sermon: "I'm not saying every woman can be the epic trophy wife of all time, like Melania Trump, maybe you're a participation trophy. . . . But you don't need to look like a butch either." As if that weren't painful enough for women, he went on to claim that the Bible gives husbands the authority to use their wives' bodies as they please: "The wife has no longer all the rights over her body, but she shares them with her husband. . . . So, whenever she's not in the mood, take out your Bible."[10] Whatever Clark's intention, his words reek of misogyny and add to the unnecessary weight many women are bearing in our churches.

The next category of sexism defined by Glick and Fiske is *benevolent sexism*, or attitudes toward women that appear positive but are stereotypically sexist.[11] They subtly position women as inferior and push women to respond in ways that are helpful to the male hierarchy or make them vulnerable. A large number of Protestant churches probably fall into this category. They are not overtly hostile but practice subtle sexism that makes women doubt their intuition and the validity of their experiences.

One of the participants in my study, Katie, reflected on her experience of this more subtle sexism in ministry:

> I get asked questions that my male colleagues do not get asked, and comments made about my clothes, shoes, hairstyle, etc. If I'm assertive, I "must be in a bad mood or angry"; if my male colleagues are assertive, they are "bold, forward-thinking, courageous." If I show too much emotion, there must be "something going on" or I'm "hormonal"; if my male colleagues show too much emotion, they are "passionate" or "stressed." It happens mostly by way of comments, attitudes, and assumptions that lead to behaviors.

The final category of sexism is *ambivalent sexism*.[12] Ambivalent sexism "is a combination of benevolent and hostile sexism. People who engage in ambivalent sexism may vary between seeing women

24

as good, pure, and innocent and seeing them as manipulative or deceitful, depending on the situation."[13] Members of the church can slip into ambivalent sexism, and the historic tendency of the church to view women through a virgin/whore dichotomy has reinforced this. This dichotomy states that women are in one of two categories: either they are "good and pure" or they are a "bad seductress." Much like hostile sexism, ambivalent sexism is not as mainstream or normative as the benevolent type.

By naming and categorizing these types of sexism, we can clarify what is at the foundation of an institution and what creates institutional sexism at a systemic level. *Institutional sexism* is when certain policies, practices, and institutional norms hold women back from further opportunities.[14]

This toxic system can lead to *interpersonal sexism* (where men treat women as less than). Interpersonal sexism shows up within individual relationships and can then inform internalized sexism. *Internalized sexism* is when women end up believing toxic messages about themselves after being inundated by damaging messages about who they are.

Defining Abuse

Sexism makes up part of a toxic environment in which abuse can more easily occur and abusers aren't held accountable for their actions or inactions. Sexism often leads to abusive relationships—but what do we mean when we talk about *abuse*? Definitions of the word include "a corrupt practice or custom," "improper or excessive use or treatment," "language that condemns or vilifies usually unjustly, intemperately, and angrily," and "physical maltreatment."[15] Certainly, countless women can attest to experiences within the church that can be described using these terms, including being treated improperly and vilified unjustly.

A good rule of thumb when determining if abuse is occurring is to first look at the power differential. Is there a power imbalance? Pastor and congregant, coach and player, boss and staff member, or even an older classmate or cousin who is looked up to—any of these positions have a place of power that can be exploited and used for personal pleasure.

Forms of abuse include emotional, sexual, financial, and physical, but I would argue that *spiritual* abuse is one of the most confusing forms—and, within the church, one of the most prevalent. But before we dive deeper into spiritual abuse, let's look at a simple definition for each of these other forms of abuse, along with how they intersect within the church. All these forms of abuse have the same foundation: an attempt to gain power and control over another person.

- *Emotional abuse* is nonphysical acts meant to assert power and control. Data collected in 2020 from the National Domestic Violence Hotline stated that 95 percent of their callers reported experiencing emotional abuse.[16] This abuse includes such things as belittling words spoken to make someone feel dumb and small in an attempt to gain the upper hand over them.

- *Sexual abuse* includes more overt sexual acts such as rape but also any nonconsensual sexual contact, including a slap on the butt or intentional brush against the breast or upper thigh. This form of abuse asserts domination and power over another's bodily autonomy.

- *Financial abuse* is a common way to have power over another person. By controlling the money, unhealthy churches exploit vulnerable people. Leaders might promise that people will get a "blessing" from God if they support the new building project, for example. Financial transparency and open communication about finances, both personally and institutionally, help safeguard against this type of abuse.

- *Physical abuse* is the most well-known form of abuse. Even the least abuse-informed communities can see bruises

26

and know something is wrong. Physical abuse is deliberate injury to a body; punching, shoving, and slapping are the most common examples.

Defining Spiritual Abuse

Just like all the other forms of abuse, spiritual abuse is about seeking power and control over another person, but this type involves declaring that God is on the abuser's side. After all, who can argue with God? Abuse advocate and author Sarah McDugal defines *spiritual abuse* as "the misuse of theology, scripture, church position, or spiritual influence to control, cause harm to, exploit, or reduce the personhood of another. At its core, spiritual abuse is any action that breaks the third commandment—where someone takes the name of God and then misrepresents his character using his name."[17] She notes this might include actions such as:

- twisting Scripture to avoid accountability
- using beliefs to gain an advantage
- leveraging spiritual leaders against another person
- silencing a person with Bible verses
- making someone believe they need you to teach them about God
- acting as the Holy Spirit on another's behalf
- excusing any destructive pattern in the name of God
- engaging in other soul-destroying behaviors

Because spiritual abuse "affects not only our body and mind but our entire worldview and our picture of God," McDugal explains, it can cause lasting damage.[18]

This abuse can be sly or blatant, subtle or fierce; there is no exact science as to what is or is not abuse, which makes it incredibly tricky when you experience it, especially from a trusted friend or spiritual guide. One of the most important items to remember when you encounter potential abuse is to trust your own body and what you feel. Scripture tells us that "your bodies are temples of the Holy Spirit, who is in you, whom you have received from God. . . . Therefore honor God with your bodies" (1 Cor. 6:19–20 NIV). God has given our bodies great wisdom, and learning to listen to our bodies is vital. This practice can help us to not be abused by those in spiritual authority, since spiritual abuse can be one of the most insidious forms of abuse. Do you feel unsafe in someone's presence? There is a reason for that; your body is warning you, and you must listen. When your pastor or counselor made that comment, what did it evoke? Did you sense you were being manipulated or undergoing an attempt to be controlled?

Author and theologian Scot McKnight has written extensively on spiritual abuse. He notes that it is "characterized by a systematic pattern of coercive and controlling behavior in a religious context," and, like McDugal, he has found that it "can have a deeply damaging impact on those who experience it."[19]

Thousands of women in my study confirmed this.

The stories I heard over the course of my research involved every type of abuse, and the offenses ranged from harmful to outright evil. The work of this book includes exposing that evil and calling spiritual communities to be better. God is truth, and the more we tell the truth and live in truth, the more fully we can experience and know God. By laying bare the evils of sexism and abuse, we can begin to heal and work to create safe churches and ministries.

TWO

Why We Must
Listen to Women

I raise my voice not so that I can shout, but so that those without a voice can be heard. . . . We cannot all succeed when half of us are held back.

Malala Yousafzai, speech at the United Nations, July 12, 2013

Ida Bauer was eighteen years old when she claimed that her father's good friend, who lived nearby, had made sexual advances toward her. Ida reported that she'd slapped him, her father's friend denied that anything took place, and Ida's own father said he didn't believe her. After this, she developed aphonia; she could not speak and literally lost her voice. In 1900, her father decided to bring her to the father of modern-day psychoanalysis, Sigmund Freud, for treatment.[1] Dr. Freud gave her the pseudonym "Dora," and one of the most infamous cases in the field of psychoanalysis was born. Dora was diagnosed as having hysteria, which was the focus of her eleven-week treatment.[2]

Dr. Freud and physician Josef Breuer had written a paper in 1893 on the study of hysteria in women.[3] At this point, hysteria was being diagnosed in women in staggering numbers, and its treatment seemed more traumatizing than the problem. Documented prescribed treatments included masturbation by the physician (yeah, you read that right) as well as "water treatments" at a resort-like sanitarium—for the wealthy—and hospitalizations and institutionalization for more unfortunate women. As Freud began listening to these women, he concluded that their hysteria was caused by unprocessed trauma, writing that "hysterics suffer mainly from reminiscences."[4] These women were suffering due to intrusive thoughts from traumatic experiences of sexual abuse, violence of various forms, and betrayal. Nothing was wrong with them, per se, but hysteria was how their bodies were processing such horrific events.

This discovery was groundbreaking, and women telling their stories led the way. Judith Herman writes about this moment in history in her fabulous book *Trauma and Recovery*: "For a brief decade men of science listened to women with a devotion and a respect unparalleled before or since."[5] These two men were helping women process their trauma narratives, and women felt heard and understood—and their symptoms were lessening.

If that were the end of the story, that would be amazing; sadly, there is more. After this groundbreaking paper was published, Freud received so much pushback and anger from those in power that he retracted his findings within a year after publication, saying that his findings "were only fantasies which my patients made up."[6] Freud betrayed the women, essentially calling them liars, because the social implications of his findings would have meant the loss of his friends and place in society. Believing the women would have meant admitting that the wealthy class had sexual abusers and predators among it, and those in power did not want that information to come out. And let's face it—these men did not want to take responsibility for their behavior personally or as a group but rather scapegoated and blamed the victims of their own violence.[7]

Does this sound familiar? Sadly, though more than a century has passed since Freud accused women of fantasizing their trauma and abuse, the church has failed to adopt a stance that is any more respectful, caring, or protective. Modern-day church leaders have continued the pattern of silencing, blaming, and gaslighting women for the trauma they have caused or allowed in their communities. It is long past time to tell the truth about what women's experiences have been like under current church structures.

Not surprisingly, most male church leaders feel an aversion to looking deeper into this issue. I've experienced this discomfort firsthand. Pursuing this truth isn't enjoyable; listening to women's experiences has been excruciating for me at times. These stories evoke many contradictory feelings: rage toward the church, compassion toward the victims, incense at the incompetence and cowardice of many church leaders, and anger at myself for the years I remained comfortably and incuriously complicit in a male-oriented system. As a man, I also feel defensive on behalf of men because I know the good-hearted intent of most (usually male) pastors. In many ways, I also feel powerless to change this system that has been entrenched in our culture. The dynamics feel so big, so complex, and so deeply embedded into every fabric of the Christian community.

Yet something needs to be done, and if I can use my privileged position as a man, a writer, a former pastor, and a therapist to listen to women's experiences and help leaders create systems that better serve both men and women within the church, this labor will be well worth the cost to me. I hope it will be to you too.

I love the church. As a kid, I was there nearly every time the doors were open and many times when they were not. I was an orphan looking for a home, and I found it in church. My goal is not to tear the church down but to build it up. I also know—as I'm sure you do—that some structures need to be torn down before they can be rebuilt.

Hearing so many painful stories from so many women has convinced me all the more that light needs to be shined into these dark corners that we seldom want to gaze at for very long. I hope they will convince you, too, that we all need to take responsibility for the unhealthy church cultures we have supported and even created. We can be part of the solution rather than continue to contribute to the problem. And this all begins with listening to and believing women.

The twenty-eight hundred women who participated in the larger study were asked to mark how they felt about certain statements on a scale of "strongly agree" to "strongly disagree." Following are a few of these statements:

In ministry I felt included in the decision-making process.
I feel like opportunities have been limited for me solely because I am a woman.
I would be surprised if I heard a sexist joke at church.
I believe sexism plays a role in my church.

Additionally, participants were asked questions including the following:

Have you ever been a victim of sexual harassment or any form of sexual misconduct while serving in the ministry?
If you feel comfortable, would you type out how sexism has or has not personally impacted you within the context of the church?

The stories I received were horrific, courageous, and jaw-dropping. I learned so much. Throughout this book, I will be referring to these answers and insights. Most of the in-depth personal stories you'll read are from my interviews with eight bold women, which formed the second part of my study.

How Pervasive *Is* Sexism in the Church?

In the section "Establishing a Common Language" in chapter 1, the first term I defined was *sexism*, in part because curiosity about its effects was where my own search for truth began. One of my initial questions when starting this research was, How many women feel the effects of sexism in their church? In other words, How big is this problem, truly?

The answer shocked me as I noted in the introduction: of those women surveyed, 82 percent believed sexism played a role in their church. That's more than four out of five! Maybe many women would not be surprised by that statistic, but I was horrified. Moreover, the questionnaire revealed that more than half of the respondents had a severe experience of sexism (1,502 women, or 54.2 percent) while only 464 (16.7 percent) had a mild experience of sexism. What follows is one of four pie charts reflecting the results of the study that I found particularly interesting.

As we've discussed, a full 82 percent of respondents agreed, to some degree, with the statement "I believe sexism plays a role

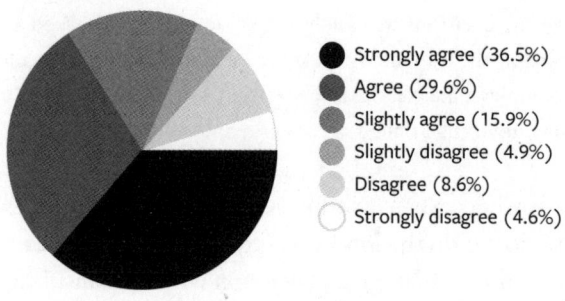

I believe sexism plays a role in my church.
2,811 responses

- Strongly agree (36.5%)
- Agree (29.6%)
- Slightly agree (15.9%)
- Slightly disagree (4.9%)
- Disagree (8.6%)
- Strongly disagree (4.6%)

in my church." Let's make this concrete. What shape do these experiences take?

Consider Hannah who worked on her church staff as a worship leader and heard the male members on staff "joking" that they could increase church attendance if they required women to wear white T-shirts to get baptized. What do you think she felt in her body after hearing that? What did she think about her own breasts? Her own worth?

Or take Elizabeth who, after sharing her testimony in church, was told by her pastor that she had the gift of public speaking—followed by that same pastor saying, "It's too bad you're a woman." Or Tamara who shared with me, "I always got paid less than the men in ministry around me. In one situation, all of the males on the worship team got paid, and none of the females were paid. Their reasoning was 'that's the way it's always been done.'" These are just a few of the blatant and not-so-blatant ways women's talents, voices, and ultimately lives are valued far less than their male counterparts.

We also need to be aware of the experiences of women like Samantha who encountered more subtle benevolent sexism, which is often more difficult to name as abusive. She described her experience working in church like this:

I had more formal education than the job required, a decade of previous experience, a supportive spouse, and even a church that said they were "egalitarian," yet at the end of the day, every single one of my decisions was analyzed, critiqued, and checked and re-checked by the lead male pastor before my ideas were ever allowed to be implemented in the ministry that I was leading. Am I really leading anything at all?

This is what sexism feels like, even when it is subtle: "Why am I not trusted to do the job I was hired to do?" The feeling that a woman could not make a final decision without consulting a male leader was a common thread throughout many of the responses to the questionnaire.

Men, does any of this sound familiar? Take a moment to consider your own church or spiritual community. Do the people there believe women can be trusted to lead? If the answer is no, why is that? Consider the part you play. What are the contributing factors that may have led you to that conclusion? How have you been socialized to think about women as the so-called weaker sex? Have you been taught that women are overly emotional and thus can't be trusted? Going back even further, reflect on your history with the women in your life, even your relationship with your mother. Relationships are complicated and have both positive and negative aspects, including those we have with the people we love most.

We must spend time in these questions and subsequent stories, and we must also make peace with them in order to untangle and rebuild a healthy, God-pleasing view of the feminine. Until men begin to engage deeply and richly with this kind of work, we will be unable to change the larger systems and structural hurdles holding women back in the church.

What Happens When Women Confront Sexism and Abuse?

You may be thinking, *Okay, sure. But what about women? They're the ones having these experiences. Shouldn't they be the ones to speak up about them?* The answer to this question, like the answers to many questions related to this subject, is complicated. The fact is, many women do speak up, or try to. But in many cases, the leadership of their spiritual community isn't prepared to receive what these women have to say.

When women experience sexism and abuse in their church environment, they often have very limited means of navigating these experiences. The path to eliciting genuine healing and transformation in their faith community is often unclear or unavailable. Many of the women I spoke with tried a variety of heroic tactics to confront the abuse—from directly confronting the perpetrator to going to the pastor or elders for help. Most who brought their experience to church leadership were dismissed as hysterical, instructed to be more forgiving, or told, "That's just the way he is, and you should get over it."

One story that stood out was from Heather:

> My now ex-husband, who was an elder in the church, was arrested on pedophilia [charges]. When I became upset that the pastor hadn't told me what he knew, an elder told me it was not the pastor's fault and he had no obligation to tell me or warn me about what he knew. This man went on to tell me it was my fault because I had married a man who couldn't keep his penis in his pants. Yes! He said this to me.

When Heather became enraged and yelled at the elder that she needed to know this information about her husband and that her children could have been in danger, the elder "went on to call members of the congregation to let them know how out of control I was and that I had yelled at him." And when Heather informed the pastor of this behavior and the comments the elder had made blaming her, the pastor dismissed her concerns, saying, "After all, he's a nice guy and does a lot of good work."

In so many instances, no matter what women did, their voices were ultimately dismissed, disregarded, and silenced. This speaks to the reality of the ingrained misogyny built into the church system and is sadly preprogrammed into many male leaders. Women cannot win if the system doesn't change. Now, for women to win does not mean men have to *lose* either. Shared power and mutuality are the goal. When power is shared, we all win.

C'mon, It Was Just a Joke

Another form of ambivalent sexism that many women face in the church is that of so-called joking, which is actually not humorous at all. Research from Dr. Thomas Ford, a psychology professor at Western Carolina University, found that "dumb blonde" and "women driver" jokes are more than just innocent banter. Ford's research results were published in 2008 in an article titled "More Than Just a Joke: The Prejudice-Releasing Function of Sexist Humor." The results showed conclusively that exposure to sexist humor "increases tolerance of discrimination"—in other words, men who tell these kinds of jokes are more likely to accept or even participate in outright sexism toward women.[8] Ford also found that "sexist humor acts as a 'releaser' of prejudice for men who have antagonistic attitudes toward women."[9] This would suggest that pastors who tell sexist jokes often have preexisting negative attitudes toward women.

In my research, 62 percent of women said they would not be surprised if they heard sexist jokes in church. These so-called jokes against women are normalized by men in power, which increases their occurrence and acceptance.

One woman wrote that "sexist jokes that were very inappropriate (and sexual) were very common. When I asked if [the male leaders] would tell less of them, I was told that 'men will be men,' and if I wanted to succeed in a man's profession, I needed to be okay with it."

This dismissal of women's gut experiences is sadly common. What men often fail to recognize, however, is that these jokes only

If I heard a sexist joke at my church, I would be very surprised.
2,811 responses

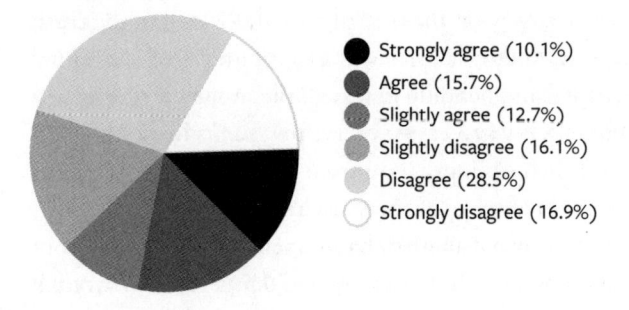

- Strongly agree (10.1%)
- Agree (15.7%)
- Slightly agree (12.7%)
- Slightly disagree (16.1%)
- Disagree (28.5%)
- Strongly disagree (16.9%)

expose what they, as leaders, seldom want to see within themselves: an internalized belief that women are less than or exist for their amusement and pleasure.

Sexual Harassment and Sexual Misconduct

Sexism may well be the most widespread problem when it comes to the way men treat women in Christian communities. By far the most troubling aspect of male behavior in the church is the occurrence of sexual abuse and harassment. From evangelist Ravi Zacharias's secret sexual abuses of women, exposed after decades of international apologetics and missions work, to the Southern Baptist Convention's sexual abuse scandal, to the sex scandal of the president and chancellor of America's largest Christian university, Jerry Falwell Jr., exposed in 2020, we have seen numerous instances of abuse break into the broader consciousness in recent years. Yet these stories of abuse of power within the Christian community are not new, and they are not rare. I found this to be true even in my own family.

My father was a pastor-turned-vice-president of a prominent Christian college in the 1980s. He also had a secret sexual life. It sounds like something from an episode of *20/20*, but it is my origin story and part of why I am so passionate about this topic. Someone from a nightclub he frequented found out who he was and blackmailed him, asking for one hundred thousand dollars on the threat of going to the local newspaper to reveal his true identity. Instead of conceding the truth, my father stole the money from the college to pay off the blackmailer. Like all lies, the truth finally came out, and my father was caught and fired. Criminal charges were filed and pending unless all the money was returned in full. Ultimately, my father lost everything to his lies and sexual secrets. My mother, siblings, and I were left to pick up the pieces and attempt to make sense of the senseless.

Not all cases of sexual abuse or harassment are so dramatic, but they are sadly common. In my research, 20.5 percent of women

Have you ever been a victim of sexual harassment or any form of sexual misconduct while serving in the ministry?

2,811 responses

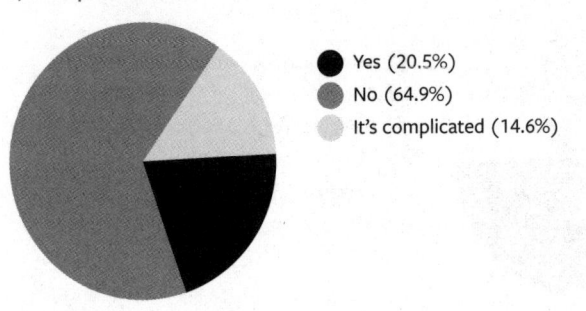

● Yes (20.5%)
● No (64.9%)
● It's complicated (14.6%)

reported suffering from sexual harassment or some form of sexual misconduct while serving in their ministry position, and another 14.6 percent answered that it was "complicated," meaning that, in total, more than one in three women reported experiencing some kind of misconduct. Further, there was a statistically significant (95 percent confidence level) association between years of ministry experience and sexism experience.

In other words, the more time a woman spends in ministry, the more likely she is to experience sexism, harassment, or abuse. That is a sobering statistic and one that should give all of us who care about and love the church pause, and it should cause us to reflect on how we can do church differently moving forward.

Limited Opportunities

With so much sexual harassment, sexist joking, and patriarchy masquerading as theological truth, it's no wonder that 77.9 percent of women felt that their opportunities in ministry had been limited due to their gender. There is a firm glass ceiling in the evangelical church that must be shattered.

Gail shared in the questionnaire about her experience with her limited opportunities as a worship leader of her church. She said,

I feel opportunities in ministry have been limited for me solely because I am a woman.

2,811 responses

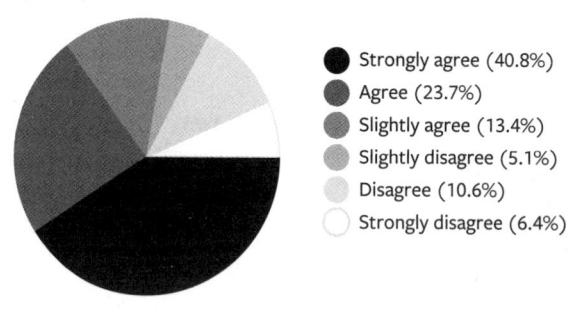

- Strongly agree (40.8%)
- Agree (23.7%)
- Slightly agree (13.4%)
- Slightly disagree (5.1%)
- Disagree (10.6%)
- Strongly disagree (6.4%)

I was kept from being hired as worship leader, although I had been "filling in" for the role for over a year, had a degree in music, and more than a decade of experience. I couldn't be hired, because I was a woman, even though leadership agreed I was doing an exemplary job and was exceptionally qualified. The man hired in my place was a far less capable musician, administrator, and music director.

Gail's experience is not isolated. The church was using her for her skills and giftedness yet had no plans to compensate her. They continued to use her until they found an average male replacement, and Gail will never forget the pain of that experience.

One of the questions in the questionnaire was "If you feel comfortable, would you type out how sexism has or has not personally impacted you within the context of the church?" Hannah answered, "I got a masters of divinity degree from Harvard, and I still could not find a church in my denomination to hire me because I was a woman, so I changed denominations so I could find a job." When we dismiss or repress the gifts of women in the church, no one wins. Gail and Hannah experienced the pain of being undervalued, and their churches missed out on the benefits of their God-given abilities. To promote a safe church for women, we all need to be aware of these extra hurdles that many women face in Christian ministry.

From Hopelessness to Hope

Many times, experiences of sexism and abuse leave little room for anything else but leaving the pain behind, whether that is separating from a specific church or one's faith system. Many women have had to exit the church entirely to find the healing they need. Beth shared,

> The sexism I experienced in the church is part of what has led me toward the deconstruction of my faith. I am no longer a member of any church, nor am I involved in any Christian ministry (though in the past I have served as a missionary and church staff member). As I worked hard to process my past, I am angry about how deeply the misogynistic views within the church impacted me (even negatively influencing the way I viewed myself). The sexism I experienced was damaging, and it is something that will take a long time to heal from.

Sadly, many women can relate to her experience. The impact of sexism and abuse can take years and years to heal from. Cameron wrote, "I left that entire church system (evangelicalism) primarily because of its sexism (and views on other issues). I hesitate to get involved in anything in my new church (Episcopalian), and, even when I do, I end up with great anxiety and negative emotions (close to a panic attack). So, I keep my distance from getting too involved." The effects of trauma still reside in these women's bodies, even long after the abuse has stopped.

After reading this chapter, you may feel a loss of hope, a great sense of despair, or both. I feel that often as well: *This elephant in the church is so big; how will we ever "take it down"? What can I do to stop this evil?* I am reminded of World War II and General

Creighton Abrams, who said of daunting tasks, "When eating an elephant, take one bite at a time."[10] Sexism and abuse are the church's elephants. The only way we can begin to dismantle this pervasive evil that permeates our sacred houses of worship is to continue to take one bite at a time. None of us can swallow an elephant whole. But every one of us is capable of taking individual bites. The elephant is no match for us if we work together.

Let's close this chapter with the wise words of author, psychologist, and trauma expert Dr. Diane Langberg:

> Understand that you cannot singlehandedly change an entire system; you are not called to do so. Yet we are to speak the *truth about our systems*. . . . When systems change, it is often little by little and usually at a great cost.
>
> When you feel overwhelmed, remember this: *people are sacred, created in the image of God. Systems are not. They are only worth the people in them and the people they serve. And people are to be treated, whether one or many, the way Jesus Christ treated people.*[11]

Let it be so.

THREE

The Historical Experience of Women

I myself have never been able to find out precisely what Feminism is. I only know that people call me a Feminist whenever I express sentiments that differentiate me from a doormat or a prostitute.

Rebecca West, "Mr. Chesterton in Hysterics: A Study in Prejudice"

Elizabeth Johnson Jr., one of two hundred women and men accused of practicing witchcraft by the Puritan ecclesiastical tribunal in 1692, was the last victim of these infamous Salem witch trials to be exonerated by the court of Massachusetts—in 2022. Over three hundred years after she was falsely accused, this woman finally had her name cleared through the work of Andover Middle School's eighth grade civics class.[1]

The witch trials were Christian courts held to condemn heresy and the use of witchcraft. What many would now call misogyny and religious extremism led to the death of twenty innocent people. Fourteen women and five men were hung, and one man was pressed to death.[2] Many of the women were targeted because they were single and had no one to advocate for them. Women who were outspoken or exhibited "hysterical" or "moody" mental states were not tolerated, even if they denied any relationship with witchcraft.[3]

Spiritual communities have historically been unsafe for women who step outside of the traditional roles men have set. If we are going to create safer spiritual communities for girls and women, we need to better understand how they have historically been treated and how that informs our treatment of women today.

The Influence of the Early Greeks

Much modern thinking about women, including negative views, has deep historical roots. Some of these negative biases can be found in the collection of writing commonly known as "the classics." We can easily hear echoes today of ancient Greek poets, playwrights, and philosophers such as Homer, Plato, Aristotle, and Aristophanes.[4]

Aristotle wrote that the female is a "monstrosity" and a "deformed male," and the playwright Aristophanes wrote in *The Lysistrata*, "Women are a shameless set, the vilest creatures going."[5] Or consider Euripides, another Greek playwright, who in 428 BC declared, "My woman-hate shall ne'er be sated."[6] Such statements are clearly misogynistic by any definition of the word. Even Homer's *Odyssey*, written more than eight hundred years before Christ, has deep misogynistic undertones.[7]

This context and background are important in understanding the origin of certain patriarchal ideas in early Christianity. The Roman culture dominant at the time was highly influenced by Greek thought as well as adding its own layers of patriarchal and hierarchical thought. Understanding the cultural context of these early interpretations of theological views is vital because it shapes the way we read and view biblical texts even today.[8] Given this, we must interpret this Greco-Roman baseline misogyny as the social context many women faced in the early church. The New Testament was written within a highly patriarchal society, yet it still miraculously contains many non- and antipatriarchal themes and aspects throughout much of the text, especially in the life of Jesus, as we'll discuss later in the chapter. Yet too often, these antipatriarchal themes have been ignored, overlooked, or outright denied as a result of that misogynistic societal influence.

Gillian Cloke, in her book *This Female Man of God*, suggests that early Christianity was impacted by Greco-Roman social norms when it became the main religion of the Roman Empire.[9] Of course, patriarchy existed before the Romans or the Greeks, and the Old Testament (written hundreds of years before the New Testament) is full of familial patriarchy, which is literally where the word *patriarch* comes from.[10] Sociology professor Dr. Catherine McKinley writes, "If patriarchy is the tool, then sexism and misogyny are its handmaids."[11] Patriarchy and misogyny are forever intertwined; misogyny sets the table, and patriarchy forces women to remain there.

If one reads the Old Testament with the goal of justifying a patriarchal view of the world, there seem to be plenty of verses to pull from. After all, women could not inherit property or even pursue a divorce (Deut. 21:16–17; 24:1–4). Wives were the property of their husbands but were considered of higher worth than slaves and concubines (Exod. 20:17). Even daughters were the property of their fathers and were married off if the price was right and, at times, sold into slavery as a form of debt relief (Exod. 21:7; Neh. 5:5). However, as Rachel Held Evans accurately points out, these stories in Scripture are the "effects of the curse that 'man will rule over you,'" not God's original design for humankind.[12]

The author of Genesis tells a story of creation that presents the first man and woman as true partners. Both are created in the image of God, and both are charged with tending to the earth God has made. . . . There are no explicit statements of a hierarchal relationship between man and woman until after the event that Christians have come to call "The Fall." . . .

It is within the context of judgment, not creation, that hierarchy and subjugation enter the Bible's story of man and woman. Where there was once mutuality, there is subjugation. Where there was once harmony, there is a power-struggle.[13]

By examining the extent to which patriarchy has infiltrated our faith systems, we can reclaim a genuine gospel faith rooted in care and love for all people regardless of gender. Patriarchy has blinded those (men) who have power, and we have lost sight of God's original intent: a vision of shared power.

The Protestant church considers the Bible the sacred text that is followed for guidance on how to live. If the influences of the system—patriarchy—that shapes our understanding of it are not studied and uncovered, then we can take in harmful and damaging beliefs alongside gospel truth, and the two can become intertwined in our hearts. This is exactly what we have seen happen repeatedly across history, and we must strive to see those influences for what they really are: patriarchy-informed cultural norms.

Complementarians keep insisting that patriarchy is counter-cultural, and that advocates of mutuality are simply capitulating to culture. But patriarchy itself is a cultural system. . . . And systems that reflect the values and dreams of only half of God's human creation (only half of God's image!) are broken. Jesus did not come to preach a kingdom that affirms these systems, but rather, to preach a kingdom that transcends them.[14]

Women in the Early Church

The experience of patriarchy by women in the church today follows women's experiences of traditional Christian patriarchy, which is, as Rachel Held Evans so succinctly captures, nothing but the same

46

old patriarchy of the non-Christian world. Both have caused many women to suffer. Beth Allison Barr details this conflation wonderfully in her book *The Making of Biblical Womanhood*.[15] Coming to terms with the marred faith we have inherited will help us sort the good from the bad. We can leave behind contaminated ways of thinking and embrace a God-honoring approach to gender and to the church.

Due to the influence of Greek and Roman culture (and patriarchy) on Christianity, Christians adopted much of the same Greek sexist, gendered, classist language.[16] North African theologian and philosopher St. Augustine, writing in the early fifth century, is historically regarded as one of the most impactful figures in the early development of Christian thought. He was the first to separate woman's nongendered soul (as an image bearer of God) from her sexual body (which was sinful).[17] This splitting of women's humanity from the image of God created an easier path to dehumanize, sexualize, and objectify women. Augustine's belief was informed by Greek values and beliefs as well as those of the Romans, who were the ruling class during his lifetime.

In the thirteenth century, Italian Dominican theologian Thomas Aquinas took Augustine's claim to darker levels, asserting that women's bodies were biologically and physically defective. He claimed they were inferior in mind, body, and will and thus must be subjected to male rule.[18] Author Becky Castle Miller says, "Instead of lovingly following the example of Christ, these men used the Bible as a weapon to control their wives. One specific way they did this was by interpreting the word 'head' in Ephesians 5:23 and 1 Corinthians 11:3 to mean 'authority' or 'overlord.'"[19] Further research indicates that

> in fact, "chastisement" of subordinates within the household was considered perfectly appropriate and even expected to a certain degree. Any word or action that defied a husband's authority was supposed to be met with punishment, and the defiant party would be expected to accept their punishment without complaint.[20]

The Protestant church began in the sixteenth century with Reformer Martin Luther and is often hailed as a story of triumph and liberation from the authoritarian bonds of a corrupt and moribund Roman Catholic church, yet the story is not that simple for women within that context. As professor and author Karin Stetina states,

> Luther's understanding of the priesthood of all believers helped promote the value of women and marriage, [but] it did not radically change women's place in the church and in the world. Women were still to be submissive to their husbands and had limited options within either of these realms.[21]

This renewed patriarchalism retains a hold on our faith communities today.

Historical Impact on the Church Today

The World Health Organization has noted that promoting "gender equality is a critical part of violence prevention."[22] Unless we accurately address the church's history of misogyny and oppression of women, our houses of worship can become the very places that unwittingly encourage or ignore abusive views and behavior. By exposing abuse, church culture can hopefully stop normalizing damaging patriarchal mindsets and create a supportive and healthy environment for all individuals.

But don't churches already offer support for abuse victims and promote healthy relationships? The answer is more complicated than it should be. A survey studying Protestant pastors' views on sexual and domestic violence, for example, found that many pastors are underequipped in regard to having the necessary resources and information to support women who are victims of violence. Also, the survey found that 74 percent of church leaders do not address domestic violence from the pulpit or appropriately support victims.[23]

A 2019 survey of church attendees in England indicated that one in four women had experienced at least one of these abusive behaviors in their current relationship: "kicked, punched, threatened with a weapon, isolated or sexually coerced." Forty percent of women reported they experienced this abuse in a current or previous relationship with their partner.[24] The rate of abused women in the church is debated, yet some research suggests there is a much higher rate of abuse (all forms of abuse) within evangelical churches that have an environment of gender inequality, which is known to drive domestic violence and abuse.[25]

A Model for Empowering Women

What hope do we have for the church and the way it engages women if the history it grows out of is so dark? Thankfully, we have an answer in the person of Jesus. In the New Testament, we see Jesus take an entirely different view of women than the culture he was part of. Against all social norms and customs, he engaged women, saw them, and welcomed them to the table.

Numerous women were part of Jesus's inner circle of followers. Mary Magdalene, Joanna, Susanna, and other women supported Jesus with their own financial and practical resources during his ministry (Luke 8:1–3). A Jewish woman washed Jesus's feet with her perfume, acknowledging and honoring him in the face of his dismissal by the religious elite (7:37–38). Jesus was a regular visitor at Mary and Martha's house and would teach and eat with both men and women (10:38–42). Jesus ignored customs and social barriers by engaging a Samaritan woman at a well (John 4:1–28). These are just a few examples of the many ways he broke the social stigma around women.

Because of Jesus and his gospel, women were drawn to the early church and its message of equality, which, as we've noted, was not normative at the time. Indeed, women were vital to the growth of the early church, such as Mary Magdalene, the apostle

to the apostles, whom Barr calls "an exemplary Christian leader—
a brave woman, who repented of her sinful life and now shared the
good news about Jesus where men lacked the courage to do so."[26]
The gospel was a radical idea that treated all people equally
and with honor. In the apostle Paul's letters to the early church,
he greets women and calls them his coworkers. Dr. Craig Keener, a
professor of biblical studies, states that "early Christians were on
the more progressive edge of gender relationships in their world."[27]
These women in the early church laid a foundation for immense
social service as the message of Jesus began to spread. A woman
named Fabiola was responsible for establishing the first Christian
hospital in Europe around the year 395.[28] Even Augustine appeared
to slightly alter his views regarding his "hatred" of women as
he matured in his faith, acknowledging that "any old Christian
woman" was smarter in spiritual matters than many philosophers
of their day.[29]

Of course, women of the early church experienced varying
levels of restrictions, depending on where they lived. In the first
century AD, women with higher status who lived in Roman cities
had more freedoms and rights than Greek women of prior time
periods.[30] Because Roman society was extremely classist, many
high-class women managed to have a strong impact on the early
church. Examples in the Bible include Phoebe of Cenchreae, who is
named in Paul's letter to the Roman church as a leader, a "deacon,"
and/or a minister "of the church in Cenchreae" (16:1–2 NIV);
Drusilla and Bernice, two Jewish princesses who heard Paul's witness while he was imprisoned by the Romans (Acts 24:24; 25:13;
26:30–31); and Lydia in Philippi, a wealthy businesswoman who
opened her home to host a house church (Acts 16:13–15, 40).[31]

As these examples prove, the early Christian church—and Jesus's friendships with women in particular—elevated women to
greater equality in a society that generally allowed them little respect. While the early church was developing, then, women were
both oppressed by the culture and vital in the church's foundation.

The church was embedded in that culture yet also made huge strides to transform it.

We, too, have the potential to transform our culture. And as with all the issues we're examining in our pursuit of creating safe churches and Christian communities, that transformation begins with looking to, and learning from, women. The historical experience of women in the church can shine much light on the church's present-day engagement with women.

FOUR

Jesus's Relationship with Women

Perhaps it is no wonder that the women were first at the Cradle and last at the Cross. They had never known a man like this Man—there never has been such another. A prophet and teacher who never nagged at them, never flattered or coaxed or patronized; who never made arch jokes about them, never treated them either as "The women, God help us!" or "The ladies, God bless them!"; who rebuked without querulousness and praised without condescension; who took their questions and arguments seriously; who never mapped out their sphere for them, never urged them to be feminine or jeered at them for being female; who had no axe to grind and no uneasy male dignity to defend; who took them as he found them and was completely unself-conscious.

Dorothy Sayers, "The Human-Not-Quite-Human"

When our son Brave was stillborn, my wife's and my own faith were decimated. Night after night, we made pilgrimage to his grave and cried out to God to bring him back to life. On the thirty-third day that Brave remained in the grave, Christy's motherly rage contended with God. She said that God only knew what it was like to see his Son in the grave for three days, and she was going crazy as death mocked her. She was our church worship leader and didn't sing a praise song for an entire year after his death; she couldn't articulate one word without weeping. Our grief was potent, but for Christy, the tragic loss tested her relationship with Jesus.

One day, after her therapy session, she begged Jesus to show himself to her—where was he when Brave died? That night, she had a dream. She was sleeping in bed and pregnant with Brave, and instead of me, Jesus was sleeping next to her as her husband. In the dream, she woke to find her abdomen ripped open and bleeding. Brave was gone, and Jesus was hysterically weeping on the other side of the bed. His hands were covered in blood. Jesus tried to explain to Christy that he couldn't keep death from taking Brave.

Christy woke from that dream with a deep connection to Jesus. She felt his humanity, his love for her and for Brave. Jesus was not just a man who couldn't understand what women suffered; he was a true advocate for women.

Jesus clearly stated his mission and purpose on earth in Luke 4:18–19: to set free the captives and prisoners of society, including the women of his day.[1] And there was indeed a need for exactly that. Many women today can surely relate. Certainly, the elevation of men over women persists, causing negative consequences that permeate our churches.

One woman in the questionnaire, Emma, shared about her church experience:

> I've wondered if God even loves me as much as he loves my husband or if God's promises still apply to me or only to men. *I keep going back to Jesus and the way he treated women,* and I remind myself that my doubts are not true. Jesus obviously thinks as highly of us as the men. The men just often don't follow his example. (emphasis added)

What Emma courageously shared is the same question many other women wrestle with: *Does God love men more than he loves me?* Yet the example of Jesus brought her back to what is true: the way Jesus lived was a reflection of God's heart to all people. Jesus brought freedom and healing to the broken, poor, and marginalized, and his ministry very clearly and specifically included women.[2] God is radically for the liberation of women.

Four Examples of How Jesus Viewed Women

Rosemary Radford Ruether, an American feminist scholar, states that Jesus "reaches out to the most marginalized women . . . those who best understand his message."[3] He also took steps to shatter social rules and assumptions that made women less safe. The Bible is filled with examples, but we'll focus on four. First, let's look at Jesus's interaction with the Samaritan woman at the well.

The Woman at the Well

John 4:1–42 is my all-time favorite story of Jesus. He modeled his mission by breaking down sexist attitudes and social strongholds regarding the treatment of marginalized women. At that time, Jewish men were not permitted to speak to any women in public besides their own family members because females were considered second-class citizens and unworthy.[4] The cultural norm at the time was to view women as unclean; as described in the ancient Jewish texts, they were "menstruants from the cradle."[5]

But conversing with a Samaritan woman was even worse. Many Jewish people expressed hatred toward all Samaritans.[6] A Jewish oral tradition recorded in the Mishnah (Shebiith 8.10) describes how Jews viewed Samaritans: "He that eats the bread of the Samaritans is like to one that eats the flesh of swine."[7] Or, as John 4:9 succinctly states: "Jews do not associate with Samaritans." Many Samaritans' experiences were marked by oppression, discrimination, and violence at the hands of the Jewish people. As such, they would have been only skeptical of Jesus, a Jew.[8]

The woman at the well wondered aloud, "How is it that you, a Jew, ask for a drink from me, a Samaritan woman?" (v. 9). But Jesus ignored social barriers, demonstrating that all people are equal.

Due to rampant patriarchy and misogyny, Jesus's treatment of women was radical within his cultural context. The church should strive toward this same goal today.[9] Professor and New Testament scholar Dr. Matthew Williams calls the Samaritan woman an "outcast within the outcasts" and also argues, "Rejected by the Jewish people; rejected by her own people; even rejected by her five husbands, she was unclean and carried shame around with her every day of her life. That is why she came to the water well—alone—in the middle of the day."[10]

Jesus invited this outcast into a deep intimacy by asking for a drink (v. 7). He shared spit with an "unclean" woman when the prevailing thought of the time was that this act alone justified spending eternity in hell. That day, Jesus performed a subtle act of revolution, breaking decades of prejudices and sexism within his own culture and beginning to change the conversation on women's worth.

Catholic priest and blogger Angela Meyer writes about Jesus's radical move that day: "The rabbinic warning against contact with women of any kind was extreme."[11] One common interpretation of this story is that this woman was a prostitute. It has been widely believed she lacked morality and, upon meeting Jesus, became redeemed and virtuous.[12] However, Meyer asserts that she could have been either widowed or divorced, and even though high tensions existed between the Jewish and Samaritan communities, both of their laws were derived from the same source, the "Pentateuch Jewish law of the pre-oral law period."[13] *The Jewish Women's Archive* states that "Jewish law on divorce is derived from Deuteronomy 24:1: 'A man takes a wife and possesses her.'"[14] If she failed to please him for any reason, he could hand her a divorce bill, upon which she would have to leave the home. Thus, for any reason, men could divorce their wives. Meyer adds she may also have been barren, and "if [she] had been guilty of adultery, we would only have to look a few chapters later in John to know what the danger to her would have been: public stoning (John 8:1–11). So, by what right do we immediately suspect promiscuity and blame the woman for her misfortune?"[15]

Whether this woman at the well was a prostitute or widowed or divorced is beside the point; the result is the same: Jesus defied social norms and prejudices to do what was most honorable for this marginalized woman. And not only did he speak with her as an equal, he also engaged with her on a deep theological level.

> The woman said to him, "I know that the Messiah is coming" (who is called Christ). "When he comes, he will explain everything to us."
> Jesus told her, "I, the one speaking to you, am he." (4:25–26)

This Samaritan woman was the first person to whom Jesus revealed his identity as the Messiah. Also, immediately following her encounter with Jesus, she was the first person to preach his gospel to others.

Rebekah Drumsta, a Christian blogger who writes about spiritual abuse and trauma, argues that Christians must allow Jesus's example to guide us into the way we live, honor women, and deeply love those who are on the fringes of our faith, despite being framed in a different manner.[16]

What if church leaders today followed Jesus's lead? What would it look like if our churches honored women rather than sexualized and objectified them? These are not unattainable goals but basic marks we can reach when we study and begin to emulate the life of our Savior.

The Woman and the Alabaster Jar

Luke 7:36–50 recounts another relationship Jesus had with a woman. In the story, Jesus went to Simon's home for a dinner party. "And a woman in the town who was a sinner found out that Jesus was reclining at the table in the Pharisee's house" (v. 37). She went home to grab her most cherished possession, an alabaster jar of perfume, and joined the party.

As she heard Jesus speak, she wept, wetting his feet with her tears. She then used her hair to wipe his feet, kissed them, and poured her perfume on them. Simon was dismayed due to the woman's societal status. Jesus reminded Simon how much this woman had done for him from the moment he entered the house. Jesus said, "Therefore I tell you, her many sins have been forgiven; that's why she loved much. But the one who is forgiven little, loves little" (v. 47). He said that Simon—a respectable, "holy" Pharisee—had much to learn from her.

The word used in the original Greek text to introduce the woman, *idou*, is also translated elsewhere in Scripture as "see" or "behold," indicating this was a woman of unusual character.[17] Was she a prostitute? The text does not explicitly identify her sin, and scholars debate as to what her profession was as "sinner" could mean she had one of several different sinful occupations "such as tax collectors, tanners, camel drivers, customs collectors, or in immorality."[18] Whatever the case, she was looked down upon. The way Jesus engaged her was countercultural and highlighted the misogynistic viewpoints that were the common cultural norm of the time.

The Canaanite Woman

Andrew Carlson, my former pastor and a personal friend, provided much of the insight in this section about the Canaanite woman in Matthew 15:21–28. This powerful story is yet another example of Jesus's engagement with women. As Jesus was traveling to a beach retreat, a Canaanite woman asked for help for her daughter, who she believed was possessed, but Jesus seemingly ignored her. The woman again asked for help, to which Jesus replied, "It isn't right to take the children's bread and throw it to the dogs" (v. 26). Jesus's response might seem unusually harsh, but as always, he had a larger plan for using the language that he did. The Canaanite woman disagreed with his response and confronted him, setting the stage for a beautiful engagement.

> "Yes, Lord," she said, "yet even the dogs eat the crumbs that fall from their masters' table."
> Then Jesus replied to her, "Woman, your faith is great. Let it be done for you as you want." And from that moment her daughter was healed. (vv. 27–28)

Matthew's Gospel identifies her as a Canaanite woman, even though there was no country of Canaan at that time. "It would be like describing a person from Great Britain as an Anglo Saxon, or a Celt, terms long since obsolete. . . . To call this woman a Canaanite is to make her a total outsider, unworthy of God's grace."[19] Jesus's disciples wanted to shun her, and even Jesus seemingly tried to ignore her, yet she refused to take no for an answer.[20] When Matthew calls her a Canaanite, "he is asking the readers encountering this story to conjure up their long history of struggle and conflict with their neighbors," which speaks to the debate that was happening between Jews and Gentiles regarding their role in the early church.[21]

Jesus was moved by her persistence and faith and was willing to be impacted and changed by this woman. Remember, Jesus first ignored her and then readjusted and told her she had a "great faith." Although Jesus first spoke sharply to her, he did so to make a much larger point: he valued women so much that he allowed them to impact him. Jesus wasn't like other so-called deities; he was fully God and fully human. This very human interaction shows a woman's impact on Jesus as well as Jesus's impact on a courageous woman.

Mary Magdalene

Mary Magdalene was the first person to discover Jesus's empty tomb. His body was missing, and she feared someone had stolen it. When Mary looked inside the tomb—the stone covering the entrance had been rolled away—she saw two angels. They asked her why she was crying.

"'Because they've taken away my Lord,' she told them, 'and I don't know where they've put him'" (John 20:13).

Then Jesus showed up! She thought he was the gardener and didn't recognize him. Jesus asked her, "Who is it that you're seeking?" (v. 15), and she then questioned if he knew where Jesus's body was taken. We often overlook the significance of this: the first person Jesus revealed himself to was a woman. Once again, Jesus was entrusting one of the gospel's most important truths (the resurrection) to a woman.

Jesus then said, "Mary," and she finally realized it was him. She exclaimed, "'Rabboni!'—which means 'Teacher'" (v. 16). Of course, she then ran back and told the other disciples that Jesus had risen, a vital messenger to the world.[22] For this reason, Mary Magdalene is sometimes referred to as the apostle to the apostles, the first person to tell the good news. This story once again shows how much Jesus valued women and trusted them with his most important messages.

Four Examples of How Jesus Valued Women

In the Bible, Jesus taught others how to engage women regardless of status or birthplace. Jesus regularly subverted cultural norms by demonstrating a mutuality with and honor of women. The stories of the woman at the well, the woman and the alabaster jar, the Canaanite woman, and Mary Magdalene are just four examples of the extent to which Jesus empowered women by allowing their voices and ideas to be heard. This undeniable truth sets the stage for the church to do the same. It's time we act as Jesus did and create safe Christian communities for all.

Moreover, Jesus demonstrated a willingness to adjust, change, and grow due to women's impact on him. Jesus modeled how to willingly surrender his power for the sake of others' liberation. In this way, he laid the foundation for more enlightened and thoughtful thinking and action regarding the status and treatment of women.

Of course, not everyone sees things this way. Many people genuinely believe God's Word teaches something different. For a long time, I did too. After a great deal of study, however, I came to believe that many key passages of Scripture have been misunderstood. A careful reexamination may reveal this to you too. Have church leaders possibly been interpreting these verses incorrectly? And if so, what can we do to bring about the widespread change our church communities need?

FIVE

Problematic Biblical Texts

People want black-and-white answers, but Scripture is a rainbow arch across a stormy sky.

Sarah Bessey, *Jesus Feminist*

Nearly twenty years ago, I was seeking a job in Seattle, Washington. I was about to move there to start my graduate school journey to become a psychotherapist. As I was a youth pastor at the time, naturally I went looking for a youth pastor gig in my new city. And over the course of a few months, I was selected as a finalist for a position that seemed to be the perfect opportunity. I could go to school full-time and work as a youth pastor on the side. In my final interview with the deacon board, they asked me to describe myself in three words. I quickly retorted, "ADD!" They loved it—I had them rolling and eating out of the palm of my hand.

I felt like I was a shoo-in for the job—until they asked one final question. "Andrew, we see you have a lot of experience in the Southern Baptist Church. Are you aware we have a woman as a pastor? How do you personally feel about that?" I froze. *Really, a woman?* I hadn't even thought about that possibility. I mean, I had heard of women in ministry positions, but it was like spotting an endangered snow leopard or a black rhino, exotic and rare in the church world I grew up in.

"Um . . ." I stuttered. "Well, um . . . okay, well, I know what the Bible says about that . . ." I tried to make another joke about myself to sound cool with the whole idea when I was truly mortified by the prospect. The entire tone of the interview changed at that moment, and the following day I withdrew my name from the running for the position. I had internalized my own sexism and interpreted a few Bible verses accordingly to reaffirm my negative views of women in leadership positions. I could not believe that a woman could teach and pastor me, a red-blooded male, because of 1 Timothy 2:12: "I do not allow a woman to teach or to have authority over a man; instead, she is to remain quiet."

This embarrassing story is nearly two decades old, and I still cringe thinking about it. I know many other good-hearted, God-loving pastors who want to please God but are unaware of their attitudes toward women and how their own internalized sexism impacts their understanding of Scripture and directly affects their female colleagues in ministry.

Scripture is meant to be used as a scalpel that facilitates healing and leads us into the painful, holy act of repentance and transformation. Yet people often use Scripture as a hammer instead, looking to pound, shame, and control those who do not meet the proposed standards set by those in power. This is abuse—spiritual abuse, to be exact.

Listen to Your Body

Before we dive deeper into the Scriptures, let's do a little emotional exercise. As you read the following two passages of Scripture, put one hand on your chest and the other on your belly, tracking what you feel in your body. Breathe deeply. One hint that a verse is being used for purposes it was never intended for is how we feel in our bodies when we read it.

The women should be silent in the churches, for they are not permitted to speak, but are to submit themselves, as the law also says. If they want to learn something, let them ask their own husbands at home, since it is disgraceful for a woman to speak in the church. (1 Cor. 14:34–35)

A woman is to learn quietly with full submission. I do not allow a woman to teach or to have authority over a man; instead, she is to remain quiet. (1 Tim. 2:11–12)

Did you feel

nauseated?
ashamed?
numb?
angry?
shut down?
like you want to throw out all of Christianity in the trash
    can?
nothing at all?

Whatever you felt, take the time to write down and process these emotions. Be kind to yourself. If you felt something negative, it's important to flush out that story through writing it down. How have those verses been weaponized against you or someone you love? Did they make you feel less than? This can be a source of great pain. Do you need to mourn how the Bible was used against you rather than for you? What would it mean to offer yourself care in the face of feeling shame or smallness?

If you read the above verses and felt nothing at all, why? No judgment; just be curious. Maybe it's because you have heard these verses so often that you have become immune to their impact or have somehow split off this part of Scripture into its own category. You may not be the feeling type of person, which is okay, but take a little time to reflect. Perhaps you don't feel because you have become used to silencing your own voice, or maybe you have some underlying pain that prompts you to remain complacent. In that case, you may need a skilled therapist or spiritual director to help you navigate through it.

Context Matters

The passages from 1 Corinthians and 1 Timothy have historically been used (and still are being used) to silence, harm, and control women, especially in the church and in marriage, often into submission to men's desires. One abusive husband I counseled years ago prayed these verses out loud in front of his wife to shame her into obedience to his absurd sexual fetish. These problematic biblical texts and many others have been weaponized against women for generations. There is no denying these verses have been harshly applied, but that's not the only problem. They've also been misinterpreted in the first place. We must study them in depth to fully understand their context, cultural meaning, and present-day significance.

There is much more to these biblical passages than merely proof-texting to fit society's (and the church's) patriarchal worldview.[1] We must understand the context of these verses so we can fully appreciate and love the Bible and each other more deeply.

Author Sarah Bessey, in her book *Jesus Feminist*, states,

> Our scriptures are not 140-character tweets; they are not an exhaustive list of rules and their expectations. They are not universal standards without context and purpose.... [These passages] are a

portion of the letters from the Apostle Paul, inspired by the Holy Spirit, written to specific people in specific cities for specific situations that had arisen.[2]

According to Bessey, these verses were intended for a certain situation; they are not universal truths for all time and all places. In other words, Paul's words in 1 Timothy 2:11–12 and 1 Corinthians 14:34–35 were meant for a certain group of women in a certain time and place, and not for all women for all time. That literally flies in the face of everything I was taught while growing up in the church.

Bessey is not alone in reaching this conclusion. As theologian Marg Mowczko writes, "Paul addresses problems and provides solutions. These passages are corrective. They are not general statements about women in the church. Paul actually loved and valued women, and they were among his ministry partners."[3] Have you ever heard *that* preached from the pulpit? That women were viewed as equals within Paul's heroic ministry? For the first twenty-five years of my life, I certainly hadn't.

At the time Paul wrote his epistles to the early churches, women were included in the work of ministry. They were invited to speak; their voices were heard. In the midst of the Roman patriarchy, women were being addressed in the church as "coworkers" (Rom. 16:3 NIV). Paul referred to Phoebe as a *diakonos* in Romans 16:1 (NIV), the same Greek word often translated as "deacon," which Paul used when speaking of Timothy in 1 Thessalonians 3:2 (CSB).[4]

The fact is Paul consistently referred to women as equals. And yet the two passages I asked you to read earlier are frequently used to try to prove the opposite. Let's take a closer look at them.

1 Corinthians 14:34–35

At the time this epistle was written, the consensus was that women in the Corinthian church, with their newfound freedom, were being loud and bothersome in the way they expressed themselves. But all women weren't the problem. Theologian Scot McKnight states, "He [Paul] is not talking about ordinary Christian women; rather, he has a specific group of women in mind."[5] Some scholars even consider the word *women* to be more accurately translated as "woman," as it may have only been one woman from the congregation that was annoying. Other scholars concur with McKnight's view.[6]

However, whether it applies to one woman or a specific number of women, this verse is not about prohibiting women from teaching in church but silencing a certain group of women in Corinth who were eager to learn but asking too many questions and disturbing church gatherings.[7] This chapter of Paul's letter concerns "maintaining order and decorum in church gatherings and Paul silences the disorderly talk from tongues-speakers, prophets, and women. The same imperative Greek verb for 'be silent' is used for each of these three groups of people."[8] Thus, this passage is not meant to convey a universal message but rather to address a specific incident at the church at Corinth.

In that same passage, Paul, as a reminder, asked the women to talk out any issues with their husbands. He encouraged women to learn to seek out answers from their partners as equals—not as submission or permission but as a conversation within mutuality. This was a very radical idea. In contrast, the normative practice taught by rabbis at that time suggested

it was better to burn the Torah than to teach it to a woman. A Jewish Rabbi would not deign to speak even to his own wife in public. Jewish men recited a prayer in which they thanked God that they were not women. The First Century Jewish historian Josephus wrote that the Law says women are inferior in all things.[9]

We must understand the context of these passages that have been used to silence half of the church. Patriarchal culture was and is alive and well, but Paul and the early church were breaking these social norms, not advancing them.

1 Timothy 2:11–12

In regard to the Timothy passage, Sarah Bessey states,

> And the word *quietly* here in the letter to Timothy isn't actually *silence*, as mentioned in Corinthians. No, the Greek word is *hes-uchia*, which means "stillness"—more along the lines of peaceful-ness or minding one's own business. It's not about talking versus not talking; it's about learning in a still way, far from meddling in other people's affairs.[10]

That changes the reading of the verses entirely: *Don't worry about others' issues but focus on yourself and still your body.* Being still is very different from silencing all women for all time!

First Timothy 2:11–12 is considered the most used passage in support of gender-based hierarchy in the church, yet it is one of the least understood.[11] In this verse, the Greek word Paul uses that gets translated as "authority" is *authentein*. The origin of the word relates to abusing one's power and/or misusing authority. This is the only time this word is used in the Bible, and it relates to a unique situation Paul was addressing directly in his letter to Timothy.[12]

Pastor Dr. Gail Wallace further asserts one cannot interpret 1 Timothy 2:12 and not apply the same type of interpretation to the verse before (women are to be silent) and verse 15 after (women are saved through childbearing).[13] In other words, if you only apply one verse to today's culture and dismiss the verses right before and after as only applying in the early church culture, then you are not using integrity in biblical interpretation but merely cherry-picking Scripture so that it means what you want it to mean.

Consistency is important when interpreting biblical passages. Wallace proffers that a personal letter written to Timothy applies to a specific situation on which he needed clarity and does not necessarily apply to the entire early church. If we do try to apply 1 Timothy 2:8–15 to silence women and keep them from teaching or preaching at any place and in any time, we then find ourselves contradicting a myriad of other passages in the Bible. Following are just a few:

- "All the women followed [Miriam, the prophet], with timbrels and dancing." (Exod. 15:20 NIV)
- "And spare my [Queen Esther's] people—this is my request." (Esther 7:3 NIV)
- "All of them were filled with the Holy Spirit." (Acts 2:4 NIV)
- "My soul glorifies the Lord." (Luke 1:46 NIV)[14]

In addition, assuming Paul meant to silence women contradicts Paul's own practice of partnering with women, numerous occasions of which are recorded in Acts—for example, Junia was "outstanding among the apostles" (Rom. 16:7 NIV). Other examples of women given prominent roles in the early church are the prophet Anna, who recognized the child Jesus as the Christ (Luke 2:36–38), and Philip's four daughters, who prophesied (Acts 21:9). And don't forget how Jesus engaged relationally with women throughout his entire ministry (e.g., Matt. 15:21–28; Luke 7:36–50; John 4:1–42).

These insights make it clear that the New Testament must be read in totality and not just small sound bites. When we stop proof-texting and read the Scriptures in their entirety, we can see they are full of messages about equality. *Equality* is not a liberal curse word; it's the longing of our Creator God: "I will even pour out my Spirit on my servants in those days, *both men and women* and they will prophesy" (Acts 2:18, emphasis added); "There is no Jew or Greek, slave or free, *male and female*; since you are all one in Christ Jesus" (Gal. 3:28, emphasis added). We are one in

Christ Jesus. God's Spirit is on us equally, and it's time we start living out our faith accordingly.

As I consider passages like the ones we've examined here, I am reminded of a sign I once saw above the toilet in someone's bathroom that read "Life is short, lick the bowl." Gross, yes, but also hilarious. I tell this story because context matters. Let's understand what we are reading so we don't misapply Scripture and do unneeded harm.

The Erasing of Women in Scripture

Problematic texts include not just those that refer to women specifically but also some that don't mention women at all. My wife points this out from the Old Testament: "They don't even mention women's names when they list lineage. A woman creates the child in her body and then tears it open to birth and still doesn't get her name mentioned." I hear her complaint. I would want my name listed if I had given birth to my child. And my wife brings up another valid point: bloodlines are matrilineal. Although all children have their mother's mitochondrial DNA, the father doesn't pass on his mitochondrial DNA to his children.[15] While scientifically we see the clear importance of the mother's biological connection to the child, Scripture doesn't present that. Somehow, men get their names listed, no matter what. Consider the following example:

Now these are the family records of Perez:

> Perez fathered Hezron,
> Hezron fathered Ram,
> Ram fathered Amminadab,
> Amminadab fathered Nahshon,
> Nahshon fathered Salmon,
> Salmon fathered Boaz,
> Boaz fathered Obed,
> Obed fathered Jesse,
> and Jesse fathered David. (Ruth 4:18–22)

No women are mentioned. When I take a second to reflect on what it would feel like not to have my name listed in biblical records if I had birthed my child, I see what my wife sees: women seem to be easily erased. Whether scholars writing this ancient text meant to omit women's names, it strongly insinuates that women are invisible. Daughters are not recorded. Mothers are not recorded.

A study in 2015 conducted by Rev. Lisa Hardin Freeman found that "there are a total of just 93 women mentioned in the Bible—and only 1.1 percent of speaking in the Bible is by women."[16] Women's experiences and voices are largely excluded from the most sacred text of our faith. Freeman "also discovered that of the 93 women, only 49 were named—and together they spoke a grand total of 14,056 words out of the 1.1 million words in the Bible."[17] What do these statistics tell us about a patriarchal culture that valued men's experiences and voices over women's? I truly believe in the Bible and the goodness of God's Word, but our interpretation and understanding of it must be rooted in the knowledge of text, soul, and culture.

My brilliant six-year-old daughter, Selah, beseeched my wife at bedtime, "I want to hear stories about girls who were heroes for God." Most of the Bible stories were about boys. Even my theologian wife hesitated at her request. After much deliberation—and believing that the stories themselves and my daughter's need to see herself represented were more important than strictly keeping to the character's original gender—my wife began to change some of the names. Is doing so factually accurate? No, but we want to foster our daughter's tender heart and imagination toward God. There are female heroines mentioned in the Bible—Deborah, Sarah, Hagar, Rebecca, Rachel, Rahab, and Esther, to name a few—but I guarantee thousands of heroic women went unnamed, and their stories have been lost.

In this chapter, we've only had time to briefly review a few problematic Biblical passages and their impact on women; I encourage you to research these and other Scriptures for yourself. Take a deep dive into the material. Find trusted theologians (perhaps beginning with those cited in this book) and read their works.

God is a God of restoration, always. If Scripture is being used to justify harm and abuse, then Scripture is being misused. One of the worst examples of the misuse of Scripture to justify evil is the enslaving of Black people for nearly two hundred years in America. Passages such as "slaves, obey your earthly masters" (Eph. 6:5 NIV) were taken out of context and used to perpetuate horrific evils. Those in power created what is now referred to as *The Slave Bible* in 1807 that removed the story of the Exodus or anything that could inspire Black people to break free from oppressive systems.[18]

If Scripture can be misused for something so blatantly evil as enslaving an entire people group, then we should not be surprised that it has also been twisted to justify subjugating and harming women. As we've seen, individual passages have been widely misunderstood and misused, and this in turn has led to problematic theology.

In the years since my young youth pastor days, I have come to understand how important it is for both men and women to bring women's stories to the forefront of our faith. Our communities are richer and more whole when we embrace, value, and make use of all people's talents and skills. Men, we can know God more fully by knowing and understanding women more completely. None of this can happen, however, as long as we remain hampered by teachings that misconstrue God's intentions for the church.

SIX

Problematic Theologies and Teachings

Now, we evangelicals have a nasty habit of throwing the word *biblical* around like it's Martin Luther's middle name. We especially like to stick it in front of other loaded words, like economics, sexuality, politics, and marriage, to create the impression that God has definitive opinions about such things, opinions that just so happen to correspond with our own.

Rachel Held Evans, *A Year of Biblical Womanhood*

Little did I realize, when I got married, the subtle beliefs I had ingested about women. Skewed theologies around submission have been the most obvious poison for my marriage. The one I am currently working on deconstructing is the amount of invisible work I assume Christy should be doing as a wife and mother. Often this plays out in my expectations of her to emotionally and physically sacrifice on our family's behalf because she is a woman. While I have given my career to righting problematic theologies like this one, it still shows up when I leave my dishes on the table, expecting her to clean them.

House chores are an easy target, but this poison also really reveals itself in our sexuality. In the church where I grew up, men commonly struggled with pornography. It also wasn't surprising to hear about a pastor's infidelity, often with no real ramifications. The teaching I heard on the subject led me to believe that how I reacted to what women wore or how they affected me sexually was their issue, not mine. Such teachings are based on male mindsets that envision a male God. The first time I heard there was something called womanist theology based on Black women's experiences of their relationship with God and their bodies, I had never even considered such a theology existed, let alone that it could be relevant to me.

When we only study theologies created by men and fail to share the pulpit with women, we can never learn about the entirety of God. Historically, the Bible has been contextualized by men, which has led to problematic theologies and painful outcomes. I have seen this time and time again in the feedback from the thousands of women involved in this project.

As we saw in the previous chapter, a proper understanding and interpretation of the biblical text is vital when developing a healthy, robust, and safe theology. But what about the commonly existing theologies that are based on poor or skewed interpretations of the text? How do they affect the church's ability to guard against sexism and abuse? The answers to these questions can be disturbing. Within these theologies, misconceptions and misunderstandings of patriarchy and so-called biblical roles run rampant.

Some of the theology that has alarmed biblical scholars regards the correlation between patriarchal theology and spiritual abuse.[1] As such, theologies of gender roles such as egalitarianism and complementarianism, as well as theological constructs such as submission, headship, authority, helpmate, marriage, divorce, grace, forgiveness, and, of course, modesty and purity have been often contested among biblical scholars.[2] The challenges inherent in some of these theologies and concepts are immediately apparent. Other constructs, such as grace and purity, represent positive ideals, but ideas surrounding their pursuit and implementation are more complicated. Let's look a bit more closely at each one.

Egalitarianism vs. Complementarianism

Though the words *egalitarian* and *complementarian* never appear in the Bible, the ideals espoused in both theologies have resulted in frequent debate among evangelicals. The debate centers on different interpretations of biblical texts regarding gender roles and submission.[3] But in many ways, "the debate between egalitarians (those who argue for biblical equality between men and women) and complementarians (those who argue for a biblical gender hierarchy that subordinates women to men) is in gridlock."[4]

Even though I worked in ministry for years, I didn't know these terms or that a debate like this even existed. But once I got to seminary, my fundamental biblical understanding was completely shaken. Only when I sat in my first biblical hermeneutics class and the professor asked the hard questions about what I brought (and what my past and present culture brought) to my reading and interpretation of the text did I start to ask myself honest questions about my theology. I had never had the courage to question such things before. As my faith grew and my understanding of God both blew up and changed, I firmly landed in the egalitarian camp, though I barely knew how to pronounce the term correctly.

The pioneering work of New Testament scholar Dr. Catherine Clark Kroeger led to the formation of Christians for Biblical Equality (CBE) in 1988, where Dr. Clark served as president until 2001.[5] The CBE still exists today and continues to advocate for mutuality and justice for women backed by biblical scholarship and authority. This is the position of egalitarians. In brief, they agree that men and women have an equal right to leadership positions in the church and that positions should be assigned by skill and aptitude, not gender.

In an egalitarian marriage, spouses are equal partners in the family and in leadership roles, demonstrating mutual submission toward each other. For example, I am better at managing people and planning events than my wife is, so any time we have a large group function or party, I am normally our team captain. I check in with my teammate (my wife) and get her input and opinions, but I take the lead because that is my natural skill. She is better at planning our family social events and managing the kids' school activities. So she is our team captain in those areas and I am her wingman, supporting her and driving the kids to all their sporting events and play practices.

The equality and mutual accountability provide a healthy system of checks and balances that a complementarian model doesn't afford to women. Though not all complementarians agree on all principles attributed to this theological view, a core complementarian belief is that only men should hold leadership positions in the church. Women may hold other positions but not those of authority over men. In a complementarian marriage, a woman must practice submission to her husband as the husband is the final authority and head of the family.[6]

The signal event behind modern complementarian theology is often thought to be the founding of the Council on Biblical Manhood and Womanhood, which crafted the "Danvers Statement" in 1987 in Danvers, Massachusetts. "This position advocates a distinction between men and women where the man has ultimate headship, authority, and responsibility in marriage."[7] This group apparently wanted to establish what was biblical and what was not in reaction to second-wave feminism, the sexual revolution of the sixties and seventies in American culture, and the growing conversation within the church concerning gender roles and equality. The Council on Biblical Manhood and Womanhood is considered responsible for coining the term *complementarianism* in 1988.

Complementarianism Limits Women's Ability to Hold Men Accountable

I am struck by how many women work so hard to submit to husbands or male church leaders who act more like adolescent boys than men. Many of these wounded men demand to be respected yet do not live respectably.

Consider the following hypothetical yet very common situation in the workplace, including in Christian churches and ministries. The male employees regularly make sexist or misogynistic comments or "jokes." The women are expected to laugh along or say nothing. What recourse do they have? Complementarianism calls for them to submit, not to challenge. Do they submit to men's authority and compromise their integrity? Or do they challenge blatant misogyny and violence against women and, in the process, "sin" by overstepping the stated boundaries of their role?

Sadly, women have been experiencing and confronting this type of sexism in the church for generations. Isn't it past time that men with privilege who hold leadership positions take responsibility to address this?

Complementarianism Limits Women's and Men's Abilities to Exercise Their Skills

Another problem with the complementarian stance is when men are required to take responsibility and lead in areas outside of their natural giftings, as I alluded to in my own marriage. Healthy relationships work when skills and talents are shared for the betterment of the team. This is mutual submission based on each other's gifts. For example, if your husband is better at cooking or construction, then you will submit to his leadership in those areas. If your wife is better at finances or interior design, then you will submit to her leadership in those areas. The most capable spouse will be the team captain, and the other spouse learns from them and follows their guidance. In a healthy egalitarian marriage, no one makes decisions in isolation. We are a team of two equal but different people with distinct weaknesses and varying strengths. Mutual submission is always practiced in the partnership and rooted in kindness. No one gets to play a gender-based trump card. About ten years ago, I heard one of my female friends say, "Well, I want the navy-blue drapes, but it really is whatever my husband decides as he has the final say." I have never forgotten this. This type of complementarian, patriarchal, hierarchy-based thinking can be very dangerous because it gives men the bulk of the power in the relationship. Being unable to make decisions about daily matters like choosing drapes can be problematic enough. But when a woman doesn't have power in the small details, it can be hard for her to act when the problem is even bigger. A woman in a relationship with a man who struggles with issues of power and control may quickly find herself in an abusive relationship that does not value her voice.

Humility and mutual submission go a long way in growing a strong and lasting—and safe—marriage. All of us who care about the role of the church in laying the groundwork for women's safety must work to change the male-defined theology that enables abuse and silences half of God's image bearers.

If you are interested in learning more about the differences between egalitarians and complementarians and the biblical authority that informs the two positions, check out a couple of my favorite resources: CBE International and egalitarian scholar Margaret Mowczko's blog (https://margmowczko.com/margs-articles /) and Dr. Beth Allison Barr's stellar book *The Making of Biblical Womanhood*.

Submission, Headship, and Authority

I was on staff at a Christian ministry when I first introduced a well-meaning pastor friend to my powerful, goal-oriented girl-friend (now wife), Christy (Dr. Christy, that is). He later pulled me aside privately and sincerely wondered, "But Andrew, don't you want more of a helpmate? You know, someone who will support your ministry?"

The role of "helpmate" my friend was referring to has to do with a more conservative reading of Genesis 2:20 that depicts Eve as a "helper" to Adam. Some scholars understand this passage to mean it is God's order for women to be subservient, assistants, and supporters of men.[8] Even at the time, I felt uneasy about his suggestion. I wanted a partner who was an equal. I had a strong personality and big goals, and I wanted someone who was strong and willing to take me on. I knew myself well enough to know I needed to be both loved and challenged, not merely catered and submitted to.

One of the ways men make women feel small is by enforcing patriarchal standards and emphasizing submission, headship, and authority. These often-misused theological constructs harm women. We must more fully understand what these concepts mean, where they come from, and how they play out in the practice of our faith. For example, *male headship* means men have authority over family relationships and includes the "traditional family model—the male breadwinner and female domestic."[9]

Remember what was said earlier about the importance of understanding a text's historical and cultural context? Let's look again at Genesis 2:20, specifically the Hebrew word *ezer*, which was originally translated as "helper." It has no historical context of subordination and is originally derived from the phrases "to rescue, to save" or "to be strong."[10]

The word *ezer* appears twenty-one times in the Old Testament. Twice it refers to women; three times it refers to people helping (or failing to help) in life-threatening situations, and sixteen times it refers to God as a helper (in eight of these instances, the word means "savior"). In this passage of Genesis, *ezer* is directly followed by the word *kenegdo*, which means "in front of him" or "corresponding to him," like a mirror image.[11]

It has nothing to do with putting another person's life or goals before one's own.

My friend's words meant that he thought Christy needed to be more about me and my goals and dreams, not about her own. I wonder now why she needed to be small so that I could be big. Are men in ministry so fragile that we need women to stifle their glorious God-given true selves so that we can thrive? Couldn't we both thrive, challenge, and encourage one another?

When I consider the church's reliance on a theology of headship, it strikes me as emotional in nature—not theological. I've noticed that many men, including myself, seem to struggle so much with insecurity that we must make others, particularly women, feel small so that we can feel less insecure. Instead of dealing with our core sense of shame and fear, we project it onto the women near us to avoid our own inner pain. This only keeps women subjugated and prevents men from growing.

If a man can take care of his own inner world now, then he will not have to try to make a woman pay his inner debts later.

Grace and Forgiveness

Grace and forgiveness are foundational to our Christian faith. The Good News is all about Jesus giving his sinless life in place of our own. But what happens when the ideals of grace and forgiveness are used inappropriately, as a form of manipulation to push victims of abuse, betrayal, or both to "show grace" or "be like Jesus and just forgive" without setting boundaries around appropriate actions?

When grace is extended independently of the other person's remorse or changed behavior, it is called "cheap grace." Cheap grace is an escape from accountability for poor behavior—words without changed action. And sadly, the church commonly uses it as a weapon against women rather than using real grace as a tool for liberation for both victim and perpetrator.

The term *cheap grace* comes from Dietrich Bonhoeffer, the courageous pastor and theologian who strongly opposed the Nazis and their evils until his execution in 1945. In his important work *The Cost of Discipleship*, based on Luke 14:25–33, Bonhoeffer states that grace and truth go hand in hand. You cannot have one without the other.[12] He goes on to say, "Cheap grace is the preaching of forgiveness without requiring repentance, baptism without church discipline, Communion without confession, absolution without personal confession. Cheap grace is grace without discipleship, grace without the cross, grace without Jesus Christ, living and incarnate."[13]

What does this mean for victims of sexism, betrayal, and abuse? For example, it is cheap grace for a husband to say, "I am so sorry, I relapsed looking at porn again" (maybe even with tears) and then do it again the following week. And it is weaponizing forgiveness for the church to simply dismiss the behavior, saying to the wife that "every man does it" and pressuring her to "forgive and move on," or telling her to just "show him grace and he will eventually change."

Many times, a man like this can be stuck in adolescence (likely due to unprocessed trauma) and act as if his actions have no consequences—and his wife who is told to "just have grace" ends up enabling an environment that is conducive to continued pornography use rather than setting boundaries to protect her own heart and the heart of her partner.

For this husband to truly change, he must feel the weight of his sin and the true consequences of his infidelity, continued deceit, and lack of integrity. This means that his real actions have real consequences.

Women, how might you respond to a partner who continues to betray you or who uses grace as a license to sin? Here are a few practical steps:

1. *Listen to your body*. Having boundaries starts with honoring your body and trusting your gut. Your body doesn't

lie—trust it. If you are not okay with one or more of your partner's behaviors, you'll feel it. Those feelings tell you that it's time to take some kind of action.

2. *Set a boundary.* It's perfectly reasonable to set a boundary around your partner's habits, such as his porn use or his abuse (verbal, emotional, physical, and any other). Don't buy into the lie that boundaries are mean. It's not shaming him to say no. He is not "just being a man." We cannot normalize toxic masculinity, sexism, or abusive behavior. That is not how men act; that is how young boys behave. As his partner, you can expect more and honor yourself in who you will be in a relationship with. Young boys do not make good marriage partners; adult men do. Therefore, treat him like an adult and say what you need to say. Tell him what you'll do if he chooses to ignore that need. For example, you might say, "I am not okay with that type of behavior, and I'm not going to continue talking when you speak to me that way. When you can talk to me differently (like an adult), I will be glad to have a conversation." Recognize that his words or behavior made you feel unsafe and/or were unkind and that you are not okay with it. Remember, your boundaries will mirror your love (or hatred) of yourself.

3. *Listen to your body—again.* By using your body as a guide and remembering that "your body is a temple of the Holy Spirit who is in you" (1 Cor. 6:19), you can then listen to what you need. Normally, you'll feel this in your gut or core. If you feel uneasy or dysregulated, ask yourself why. Share your fears with a trusted friend, therapist, or spiritual director. But lean into the uneasiness rather than away from the feeling. For example, if your husband relapses and is being open, honest, and repentant about it, that is very different from if he has been lying to you for the last

decade and you just caught him sexting or looking at porn after he told you repeatedly that it's not an issue. Your body and the voice of God will guide you as to the next steps. Do you need him to leave for a week or a month? Do you need him to reach out to a trusted friend or a licensed therapist? Do you need to have a therapeutic or trial separation? What do you truly need to feel safe after such betrayal? If your partner is ready to become trustworthy and worthy of your respect, he will make the proper effort to become a good and safe man you can depend on.

4. *Expect your partner to listen and change.* Healthy men will react in a healthy way to boundaries. They may not like them, and that's okay, but they will be reflective rather than merely reactive. They will put your safety over their comfort. If they choose not to do that and continue in their abusive ways, then you need to first get to safety and then make plans to remove yourself until he can make lasting changes.

Setting and keeping boundaries is indeed painful and difficult, but that is what living in truth and love looks like. You want the best for your partner (love), and settling for what he continues to participate in (false intimacy and running from deep wounds that are being eroticized) is not accountability or love. It is not helpful for you to continue to "show grace" in a way that does not demand a changed life.

And yet churches often encourage women to do exactly that.

While conducting my study, I heard again and again from abused women that they were pressured to forgive their abuser and that if they didn't, it was their fault if the abuse continued. Kristin shared, "After my husband was abusive and porn-addicted, I was told to forgive, that my 'anger would cause him to do porn more, so I shouldn't get angry.' Since I was a Christian for longer, I should set a better example."

Do you see what those who counseled her did there? They told Kristin not to feel angry or else she would make her husband's porn use worse. They did not hold her husband accountable for objectifying and abusing women but blamed her for not being forgiving enough. And they told her not to feel. The truth is, she should not only feel angry but also enraged, betrayed, heartbroken, and grief-stricken. Rather than focusing on the abuser and his abuse, they weaponized forgiveness, which sadly happens all too often.

Leaders who want to do better need to recognize what weaponizing forgiveness looks like so that they can avoid doing it. So what does it mean?

- Pressuring the victim of abuse to forgive quickly without proper grief or repentance from the perpetrator for the pain they inflicted.
- Misquoting Bible verses on forgiveness to manipulate the victim into bypassing the harm.
- Prioritizing forgiveness of the abuser instead of sitting in the harm and the suffering with the abused. The leaders want to make the problem the victim's, not the abuser's.
- Focusing on doing, not feeling; checking off the box and doing what's supposedly right in front of others. Think of the Pharisees in Jesus's day.
- Moving on without resolution. That is the highest priority. It's not about actually being present with the victim in her heartache but about telling her to get over it as quickly as possible so the leaders no longer need to feel obligated.
- Convincing the community to agree with the leaders to pressure the victim into moving on. If others pressure her, that will fix her; in other words, the victim is the real problem.

Forgiveness is important for one's own mental health, and God calls us to forgive. But forgiveness comes in waves and should not be coerced or pressured. Forgiveness takes time, and that's okay. Forgiveness also doesn't mean instant reconciliation or a lack of boundaries but quite the opposite. And sometimes reconciliation is just not possible.

Earlier, I mentioned my father's secret life. I'm still in the process of forgiving him today. Sometimes I love my father and forgive him; other times what I feel is closer to hatred. Both are acceptable. These feelings need to be engaged rather than judged. Both anger and forgiveness are blessed, meaning they are just feelings in our bodies. I must make peace with my ambivalent feelings and the fact that I fluctuate between love and hate and between forgiveness and unforgiveness toward him. Both positions make sense, and the sooner I can have compassion for my unforgiveness, the sooner I can move deeper into releasing the power that my unhealed wounds from my father have over me.

Modesty and Purity

I saw a recent post on "modesty" that exposed a church leader's view of women and his pornographic mindset—in which he blamed women for his own propensity to sin and objectify their beauty. For example, he noted how selfies of women posting on social media about their weight-loss journey and pictures of themselves working out, at the beach, and so on are not appropriate because they could make men "stumble."

I have some compassion for this opinion because I was that man fifteen years ago. At the time, I was struggling with objectifying thoughts about women's bodies, and it was much easier to make my propensity to sin the women's issue rather than my own. Simply put, I blamed the object of my desire instead of wrestling with the desire itself. By blaming a woman for wearing a certain outfit, I did not have to reflect on my own deep shame or history of pornography abuse.

This reminds me of Adam blaming Eve and attempting to escape responsibility for his own poor choice to defy God. "The man replied, '*The woman you gave* to be with me—she gave me some fruit from the tree, and I ate'" (Gen. 3:12, emphasis added). Adam worked hard not to take ownership of his own sin and looked for any scapegoat he could find, just like the man who wrote that post claims his lust is the women's fault for posting pictures of themselves.

No, sorry, this couldn't be more incorrect. Every woman and every man has the privilege and responsibility of deciding for themselves how much of their body they feel comfortable showing—and none of that is dependent on other people's standards.

A woman's body is not the problem. But how a man chooses to engage her body *can* be problematic. Theologian Marg Mowczko writes about the early church's view of modesty:

> The first-century church strived to be inclusive of Jew and Gentile, free and slave, male and female (Gal. 3:28), and there were some efforts to be egalitarian. A degree of equality was achieved wherever and whenever the Holy Spirit was moving powerfully and freely (e.g., Acts 2:44). However, it was not always easy to maintain. So, Paul taught that distinctions that might lead to tensions and divisions should be avoided.[14]

One of these divisions was due to the way wealthy women were flaunting their expensive outfits, jewelry, and hairstyles. This was causing tension with the other women in the church, many of whom were poorer and/or enslaved.

What does the New Testament say about women covering up and dressing modestly? Practically nothing. No woman is ever described by her appearance in the New Testament. However, it is evident that some women in the Ephesian church were wearing expensive clothes. Paul's instructions about modesty in 1 Timothy 2:9 were written in response to these problematic rich women who were wearing luxurious clothing, had fancy hairstyles, and were flaunting their wealth.[15]

Mowczko makes a further point about our modern-day sexualized interpretation of the word *modesty* and the apostle Paul's stance:

[First Timothy 2:9] has nothing to do with covering up cleavage or thighs. . . . Paul tells Timothy he should encourage or appeal to "older women as mothers, and younger women as sisters, with absolute purity" (1 Tim. 5:2). Paul places the onus on Timothy in how he should relate to women and maintain moral purity. There is no caveat here that passes some of the responsibility of Timothy's purity onto the women in the Christian community at Ephesus.[16]

Clearly, Paul gets it. This is about personal responsibility, not about blaming women. When Paul wrote about the concept of modesty, he was referring to women flaunting their material wealth in a way that caused community discord. It was not about their body parts.

What does this look like in practical terms for men? I think of my response to beautiful Mt. Rainier in Seattle as an example. Seldom is it out in its fullness, yet during the three months of sun and clear skies, it is stunning. The mountain towers over the city and is awe-inspiring. I find its beauty to be glorious and evoke worship toward the God who created it. Mt. Rainier's beauty cannot be taken with you; even pictures can never do the mountain justice. This is an example of a posture of honor toward beauty we experience—it leads us to God.

Now compare this to a man who sees a woman jogging on the street. He looks her up and down and consumes her beauty without her consent, using her body for his own selfish pleasure and arousal fulfillment. Instead of honoring her, he objectifies and devours her, which will only lead to further death and heartache for him. Which posture do you personally demonstrate when you see beauty? Which posture do you think the man who wrote the "modesty" post demonstrates?

Men, may we have the courage to engage our own arousal of beauty. (Remember, arousal is not bad; we are meant to be aroused by beauty. It is what we do with that arousal that can be an issue.) It is time for us to take full ownership of our own relationship with beauty and how we engage and scapegoat women for our unaddressed brokenness. It is well worth the high cost.

Marriage and Divorce

Another common teaching in churches that fail to create safe communities for women is an ideology known as "marriage no matter what." This teaching can be harmful to all women, but it's particularly devastating to those who have been victims of abuse and those whose partners are in the process of grooming them—that is, making them vulnerable—for future abuse. The idea behind "marriage no matter what" is that a marriage should be preserved at all costs, and that, regardless of circumstances, leaving a marriage is always a sin. This damaging ideology is a salvation fantasy for many church leaders. (The unconscious thought is "look how many marriages are thriving under my leadership" versus "if marriages break up under my leadership, I must be a bad leader.") This twisted ideology keeps women bound to violence. A woman from my study, Beth, shared her experience with this message: "I can't tell you how many times I heard the head pastor say from the pulpit, while teaching about marriage and submission and things of that nature, 'They might not have been the right person before you married him, but you married him. And so, they are the right person now.'"

This ideology has so many casualties, so many war-torn women who tried and tried and tried to make their marriages work, who compromised their bodily autonomy, who gave and gave and gave, who surrendered and submitted to insecure, abusive, and theologically misogynistic men for the sake of the marriage only to be left isolated, alone, and, many times, ostracized from the only community they have known.

Another woman, Greta, shared that "I've been told that the solution to marriage problems in the church is for women to 'cook more and have more sex.'" I promise you; no amount of steak dinners or sexual favors will make a husband honor his wife and treat her as an equal. Marriage cannot heal abuse, and, in many cases, it merely provides a safeguard and protection for an abuser from being held responsible for his toxic behavior.

My mother was one of those women. As I previously mentioned, for nearly twenty years my pastor father cheated on my mom without her knowledge. Finally, after someone blackmailed my father, it all came out. My mother stayed for another year while my father got help, but nothing changed. She was ultimately forced to leave with my siblings and me to seek safety three states away near her parents.

A few years later, my mom, my siblings, and I were in a stable place and began going to a church where we started making friends and feeling more at peace. One of those supposedly well-intentioned older ladies with zero tact approached my mother, saying, "Your kids need a father!" My mother didn't respond. For years, she never told the truth about my father's lies or infidelities but instead chose to remain silent and supportive. She believed the dangerous message of "marriage no matter what" and "God hates divorce more than abuse." She remained legally married to my father for another twenty years. It took her that long to feel free enough to get a divorce and start dating again in her sixties.

"Marriage no matter what" negatively affected my mother, leaving her bound to a man who had broken their marriage covenant many years earlier and was unwilling to change. This hurt her emotional and spiritual health, which also had a negative impact on my siblings and me.

There are many misconceptions about divorce and its negative impact on children, such as that children's lives will be utterly destroyed or that it will totally mess up their future relationships. But a toxic, dysfunctional, abusive marriage will always do much more harm than a divorce ever could. Gretchen Baskerville's book *The Life-Saving Divorce* is a vital resource on this topic. She breaks down the mindset that is needed to create healthier relationships. According to her, a lifesaving divorce is one undergone in order to find relief from a marriage with a pattern of infidelity, sexual immorality, physical or sexual abuse, chronic verbal and emotional abuse, serious addictions, or abandonment/neglect. These divorces are not due to boredom, finding someone else, feeling unfilled, missing partying, and so on but rather happen "when every stone has been turned and every effort has been expended."[17]

The need for lifesaving divorces—and for people to decide for themselves what is lifesaving to them—should be evident. Yet the stigma of divorce in the Christian community creates a phenomenon where folks who have already endured so much pain and heartache are retraumatized, relegated to second-class citizens, and branded as damaged goods or failures or both. This trend of indelible marking is beginning to change culturally both inside and outside of the church, but we have much further to go to truly begin to treat the brokenness of relationships with honor, tenderness, and care.

Author John Pavlovitz says it well: "I refuse to be a Christian who is generous with damnation and stingy with grace."[18] My mom certainly deserved more grace and less damnation. She should have received applause for simply getting out of bed in the morning, for tying her shoes, and for the miracle of getting three fully clothed kids to church! Yes, this victory needed to not only be seen and acknowledged but also wildly celebrated. Instead, my mother heard hushed comments from behind our pew such as, "I can't believe she let her child wear shorts to church!" My mother had suffered the nuclear bomb of my father's infidelity and two decades of secret behavior and addiction, but somehow, because she allowed us to wear shorts to church, we were all destined for the Bad Place. It was truly an adventure in missing the point.

The stigma of divorce in Christian communities unfairly impacts women more than men. Typically, women face financial instability if they have not been the primary income earner, and many times they face the challenge of childcare if they have been the main caretaker. If we are to create safe communities for women, we need to let that stigma go. That doesn't mean taking up some antimarriage feminist mantra of "Let's take to the streets and liberate all oppressed women from the bonds of patriarchy!" (although the latter doesn't sound all that bad). Instead, this is a call to hold men accountable for horrific behavior and not allow them to hide behind the institution of marriage as a pass to act childishly and to use women as scapegoats for their misbehavior.

If a husband abuses his wife, cheats on her, or treats her poorly, then yes, she will leave him—because that is not how you treat someone you love; that is how you treat someone you hate. God loves us and hates abuse. Like men, women are bearers of God's image, and any man who abuses one is abusing God too. Any leader seeking to build safer communities has the responsibility and privilege to embrace teachings that make it easier for women to stop this abuse—for the sake of both men and women and for the community.

God Is Not Male

I once posted this statement on my social media page: "God is not male." You would have thought I'd set off an atomic bomb within people's souls. I received over a thousand comments from angry people protecting God's maleness and apparently all the sacredness of Scripture. Here are just a few of them:

False teacher (prophet)

Bigot

You idiot

You're a doctor?

You are only saying this to get "likes."

Liberal

Woke

Blasphemer

You're not a Christian.

Heretic, heretic, heretic

You get the idea. The internet can be brutal. Yet when I look beneath my bruised ego, I see that this hit a nerve. The energy that came at me is curious, to say the least. Something here is worth looking into. Why do so many Christians need God to be male to be okay?

Let me clarify what I mean. God is neither male nor female. God transcends gender; God is Spirit. Of course, yes, Jesus came to earth as a man. But Jesus's embodiment during his time on earth doesn't signal a larger gendering of God. Even infamous patriarchal pastor John Piper states, "We should not think of God the Father or the Holy Spirit as men. They are spirit, not biological."[19] Yet Christians seem to cling to the idea that God is a man and God is in charge, thus men are in charge. So at the end of the day, many Christians believe men are better than women, consciously or not. This sets up a hierarchy of gender that God did not intend but that sin brought into the world. In other words, God's intent was not male dominance over the female but shared power as coequals (Gen. 3:1–24). As mentioned in chapter 3 in this book, patriarchal dynamics between Adam and Eve began *after* the fall of humankind when sin entered the world, not before.

The misunderstanding that God is male is rooted, in large part, in the weaknesses of human language. Theologian Marg Mowczko says it better than I can regarding God's perceived maleness:

> Despite the fact that God is Spirit and should not be understood or defined in terms of sex or gender, many of us believe, either consciously or subconsciously, that God is somehow male. This masculinist view is exacerbated by the fact that, in the majority of English translations of the Bible, God is only referred to with masculine pronouns, such as "he." The reason God is referred to as "he" is largely due to the limitations of language. There are no divine or appropriate non-gendered third-person singular pronouns in the biblical languages that we can use when talking and writing about God. So we are limited to the grammatical genders of masculine and feminine in Hebrew, and masculine, feminine and neuter in the Greek.[20]

No gender has the corner on God. I love the fact that God's mysteries are much bigger than I can comprehend. It would be quite a shame if any human person could fully understand God. Let's rest in the divine mystery and know that God is a God for all of us; we all bear God's image uniquely and particularly (Gen. 1:27). That includes women just as much as it does men.

Still unconvinced? Let's look at a list of just some of the female images of God found in the Bible compiled by the Women's Ordination Conference, a group from the Roman Catholic Church.

Genesis 1:27—Women and men both created in God's image
"Humankind was created as God's reflection: in the divine image God created them; female and male, God made them."

Hosea 11:3–4—God described as a mother
God: "Yet it was I who taught Ephraim to walk, I who took them up in my arms; but they did not know that I healed them. I led them with cords of human kindness, with bands of love. I was to them like those who lift infants to their cheeks. I bent down to them and fed them."

Hosea 13:8—God described as a mother bear
"Like a bear robbed of her cubs, I will attack them and tear them asunder."

Isaiah 66:13—God as a comforting mother
God: "As a mother comforts her child, so I will comfort you; you shall be comforted in Jerusalem."

Isaiah 49:15—God compared to a nursing mother
God: "Can a woman forget her nursing child, or show no compassion for the child of her womb? Even these may forget, yet I will not forget you."

Isaiah 42:14—God as a woman in labor
God: "For a long time I have held my peace, I have kept myself still and restrained myself; now I will cry out like a woman in labor, I will gasp and pant."

Psalm 131:2—God as a mother
"But I have calmed and quieted my soul, like a weaned child with its mother; my soul is like the weaned child that is with me."[21]

What a beautiful and inspiring list of Scripture verses, revealing God's unique posture toward all humanity. Taken together like this, they clearly convey a potentially faith-transforming and church-transforming truth: God was never intended to be viewed as solely or even expressly male.

As we've seen, problematic theologies have created chaos within Christian homes and churches. Close examination of several of these reveals that they deserve to be exposed for what they are: at best, suggestions that uphold patriarchal, cultural strongholds that are not God-pleasing, and at worst, toxic and harmful teachings that have truly hurt women, unfairly demonized them, and subjugated half of the population. These theologies have also led to the traumatization and abuse of countless women. How did this happen, and what does this look like? Let's examine the situation more closely. Understanding the complexities of trauma and abuse is vital to creating a safe church.

SEVEN

Understanding Trauma and Abuse

Dear God,
   Sustainer of life, redeemer of what is broken.
   I need you. I need you to be close by; my heart and body are weary.
   I'm exhausted from the pain of my partner's projections onto me. His insecurities, unfair judgments, entitlement, and lack of healing, his own wounding—I can no longer bear it.
   My God, come, be with me; I am so tired.
   Give me the power to say, "No more!" Give me strength and safety if I need to walk away for good.
   May I stand in the glory of bearing your image, knowing my deep goodness, beauty, brilliance, and power. May I know that I am Queen.
   May I have the courage to step away from the position of "saving" my partner, knowing that "saving" is your work, and your work alone.

Help me both to rest and fight. To rest, knowing the fullness of my identity, and to fight, warring against the evil that is trying to steal, kill, and destroy me.

Yes, God, sustainer of life, redeemer of what is broken.
Let it be.

Andrew J. Bauman

Claire reached out to me via email. She was married to an insecure and abusive Christian man named Todd. Todd would never admit that he was abusive. He told himself he was a good provider, as he worked a regular nine-to-five job as an accountant, and he was a good, honest, churchgoing man. Claire homeschooled their four kids and managed the home. Todd controlled the family finances and how Claire spent any money. She had a hundred dollars a week to spend on groceries for the entire family and fifty dollars a month for any personal items such as clothes, a haircut, and self-care.

Todd had isolated her from family and friends, convincing her that they were not godly influences on the kids. He regularly commented on Claire's weight and body, making her very aware of what she ate when he was home. She had to be ready to give him sex on demand, or else he would recite Bible verses about her not "serving him." She was very afraid Todd would "take the kids away" and "make her homeless" if he found out she had contacted me. She only came for one session, while Todd was at work, and she had secretly saved up the money over the last few months to pay my counseling fee.

During our session, she told me about the condition of her marriage and their lifestyle. She was fearful, depressed, trapped, and angry. She wanted to be a "good Christian" but felt used sexually and like she was dying inside; she did not have a voice in her marriage. She reported having regular headaches and migraines, panic attacks, digestive issues, and a thyroid imbalance. They had already spent over a year in counseling with their pastor, and still,

Claire's body was screaming for change. Todd was not open to further counseling.

I reassured her that what she was feeling was very normal, given the environment she was living in. I also informed her that what she was experiencing was a form of intimate-partner violence. Though Todd never physically hit her, he controlled every aspect of her life, and she was not free to be herself or just be a human being.

Many times, emotional abuse can be deeply devastating because it is so subtle and thus easier for the victim to dismiss their body's reactions. Emotional abuse can feel like a thousand pinpricks; on their own, they are annoying but easy enough to manage, but when put together over years and years, a victim will eventually bleed out and die if they do not attend to them.

Many victims of abuse long for an abuse that is "more visible" so that they can feel justified in leaving. Claire was no different. I informed her that her body was telling the truth, that she needed support, and that God hated abuse. We reviewed the power and control wheel of domestic violence, and I gave her all the available resources and safety planning information possible. And then she left my office.

Two years later, I received another email from Claire, requesting another session. I had thought of her many times since that first session, wondering if she was okay. When she walked into my office, I barely recognized her. She was glowing and stood tall and powerful. I immediately told her what I was experiencing in her presence, and she filled in the blanks. She had reached out to the free resources I provided, beginning by getting the help of a domestic violence coach and advocate to make a firm safety plan for leaving Todd. She was able to remain safe and eventually win a majority of custody over their children. She said, "He no longer has power over me and is no longer my god." Her kids were thriving. After about a year, she found an incredibly kind, abuse-informed church community and reclaimed her faith.

Ava came into my office longing to please God yet at the end of her rope with her abusive husband. She presented small and timid, hesitant to speak her truth, and awkward when alone in the presence of a male therapist. But she knew something needed to change, and she was willing to try to find that change with me. She reported feeling less than while in her husband's presence. He knew it, knew his power over her. He regularly reminded her of her subordinate role, reciting Bible verses to get her to comply.

As she and I developed a trusting therapeutic relationship, she began to further question his treatment of her and to develop a stronger sense of self and identity in who God called her to be. She grieved all that she had lost while married to this man and knew she could be free. I began to reflect with her on what their nearly six-year-old daughter was learning about relationships from watching their marriage.

Ava finally had enough and began creating boundaries. She stopped allowing the Bible to be used as a weapon against her and began to stand up as an equal in her marriage. This stand actually made her marriage worse, which I had warned her would probably happen. Though she was never in physical danger, Ava experienced verbal, emotional, and spiritual manipulations. They increased as her husband desperately looked for any way to control her. He knew he was losing the power he had over her, and he hated it. Ava continued to stay resolute and eventually he gave up, not on the marriage but on trying to control her. He came to me, and I connected him with his own therapist who could help him with his issues. This is one of the few stories where both partners decided to do their own healing work, and the marriage was eventually saved. Many times that is not the case because ultimately abuse destroys, and for any relationship to be healed, the abuse has to be fully addressed and eradicated.

General William Sherman said "war is hell," and I completely agree.[1] I would also say abuse is a kind of war. As a therapist, I can further attest that the hell a woman bears by living with an insecure, defensive, and reactive partner (or even a church) can leave her with post-traumatic stress disorder (PTSD) similar to that of a veteran returning from the hell of war.

This observation has led me to an intriguing possibility. What if we began to treat women who have suffered abuse both within their own homes and within church contexts like we do veterans with PTSD?

A recent article in *US News & World Report* cites the following U.S. Department of Veterans Affairs statistics:

> About 11 to 20 out of every 100 veterans (or between 11 and 20%) who served in operations Iraqi Freedom and Enduring Freedom have PTSD in a given year. . . . About 15 out of every 100 Vietnam veterans (15%) were currently diagnosed with PTSD when the most recent study of them (the National Vietnam Veteran Readjustment Study) was conducted in the late 1980s. It's believed that 30% of Vietnam veterans have had PTSD in their lifetime.[2]

Those numbers related to military veterans are startling. When we look at the global statistics on male violence against women, the numbers are even worse. The World Health Organization reports that "about one in three (30%) women worldwide have been subjected to either physical and/or sexual intimate partner violence or non-partner sexual violence in their lifetime."[3] They go on to say that "almost one-third (27%) of women aged 15–49 years who have been in a relationship report that they have been subjected to some form of physical and/or sexual violence by their intimate partner."[4]

Based on a global female population of more than four billion women, from my rough calculations, there could be more than one billion women worldwide suffering from PTSD due to physical or sexual abuse. Yes, more than 1,000,000,000! And that doesn't include emotional, spiritual, financial, or even verbal abuse. I assume that number would be far higher if we included all the different forms of abuse where people assert power and control over another.

As a therapist, I've seen over and over again that all kinds of abuse leave women in a state of trauma. Dr. Gabor Maté says, "The word trauma has Greek origins and means *wound*. It's a psychic wound that leaves a scar. It leaves an imprint in your nervous system, in your body, in your psyche, and then shows up in multiple ways that are not helpful to you later on."[5] These deep wounds need skilled attunement, care, and wise guides to help usher in the proper restoration.

Men, this is the world we are living and leading in: one in which abuse and trauma are widespread, even common. This is who we are attending church with: women who have been abused and traumatized. Trauma and abuse cannot be entirely taken out of our world, at least on this side of heaven. The question is, How are we going to deal with them?

Our individual selves and the organizations we lead and are a part of must become trauma- and abuse-informed. This means everyone needs at least a basic grasp of what trauma and abuse are and how they affect our minds and bodies. We must understand the importance of not retraumatizing someone by what we say or do, and we must comprehend the basic complexities of abuse dynamics, including power and control and how someone who went through an abusive relationship might hear or understand what we are communicating.

Are you living a trauma-informed life? Are you attending an abuse-informed church? If you think you are, consider this test: ask yourself how many sermons you have heard on abuse while attending your church. If it is clearly understood that nearly one-third of your congregants have a shared experience in life, don't you think the topic should be openly discussed from the pulpit? And yet, this rarely happens.

There is something covert and dark about abuse. I truly believe that the evil one is at play, attempting to "steal and kill and destroy"

(John 10:10). His goal is to silence us on the topic of abuse. Why? Because if we talk about it, we might do something about it. Instead, he nudges us to remain quiet. What a perfect way to steal, kill, and destroy—then isolate—abuse victims so they feel utterly and uniquely broken. He then makes abuse such a taboo topic of discussion in the church and throughout our lives that we say nothing at all.

We must speak up and speak out. I hope to bring more awareness to Christians so that we take women's trauma and the systems that harbor it more seriously. We must live in a way that shows more fully and deeply the love Christ has for our world and for those who are orphaned and widowed through abuse issues. Whether we are abuse victims ourselves or want to live more abuse-aware and compassionate lives, we must learn the impact of abuse and know what to do to change it.

The Impact of Trauma and Abuse

Our bodies are not meant to bear abuse in any form. Those of us who have encountered any of the types of abusive behaviors will probably suffer lasting physical impact. Trauma researcher Dr. Bessel van der Kolk summarized it nicely in his book *The Body Keeps the Score*. Dr. van der Kolk and another psychologist, Dr. Jonathan Shay, have worked extensively with veterans with severe PTSD. They and their contemporaries have found that because "the body kept the score," the key to healing these stored traumas was also found within the body.

> We have learned that trauma is not just an event that took place sometime in the past; it is also the imprint left by that experience on mind, brain, and body. This imprint has ongoing consequences for how the human organism manages to survive in the present. Trauma results in a fundamental reorganization of the way mind and brain manage perceptions. It changes not only how we think and what we think about, but also our very capacity to think.[6]

As we've already explored, historically the church has not honored women's voices or experiences. But the prevalence of trauma and abuse in the world will not allow us to remain silent and unsupportive any longer. We must learn to listen to women who have been harmed and whose bodies have been marked.

If I have learned anything from the last three years of researching women's experiences in the church, it's that women who have been harmed have a lot to teach us about what they need to stay safe and thrive. For those of us who are male and/or have held positions of leadership, it's uncomfortable, to say the least, to learn from these women because their pain often points us right back to ourselves. In other words, if we take these women's stories seriously, then we must look deeply at how we have been complicit in the system that has exploited women and protected men. If I want to stay comfortable and in charge, I won't listen to women who have been harmed by the very system that most benefits me. This is called *privilege*, and many men have it. Since certain dynamics don't necessarily happen to us personally, we don't think they exist. But the women of the church have said otherwise.

One woman from my study, Sandra, shared, "I believe I would have escaped an abusive marriage much sooner if I'd had proper acknowledgment and support from the church." She further related that her abuse was condoned by the very community meant to protect her. It felt like her church completely missed her experience, putting the importance and focus on her marriage rather than on her safety.

Another participant, Brooke, shared her horrific experience of seeking help from her pastor for her abusive marriage.

When I sought help from my pastor with my abusive marriage, it was immediately discovered that I had set a recent boundary of no sex with my husband. (This had been about seven or eight weeks. During this time, he threatened to leave me every other day, and it was only a few months after my youngest was born.) I could not

106

bring myself to be so vulnerable with him when he was telling me he wasn't sure if he was committed to me. My pastor told me he would not go any further in counseling until I resumed sex, citing how, as a woman/wife, my "breasts were to be available to him at all times." The lesson I learned was that my voice, my safety, my judgment, my spiritual character, my spiritual gifts (discernment, wisdom), etc., held no value, only my availability as a sexual object, because that was my ultimate role as a Christian woman.

This pastor told Brooke to violate her body and betray herself, her body, and the voice of God inside her, guiding her boundaries. By all indications, he didn't understand that her husband's behavior was abusive or he didn't care or both. He certainly gave no sign of understanding the impact abuse and trauma can have on a woman's life. And in this way, he became a source of abuse himself.

What makes this abuse so egregious is that it is coming from a spiritual authority who, in a sense, represents the voice of God in Brooke's life. This pastor was advocating for Brooke to be more porn-like, not Christlike, in her marriage.

Given examples like these, it is no wonder so many women are hurting and no wonder many have reported that their real healing only began when they went *outside* the church to get the proper counsel from a licensed therapist. We must equip pastors, elders, and counselors to be trauma- and abuse-informed so that we can mitigate the harm that has happened to Brooke and thousands of other women in similar positions.

Equipping Church Leaders

Part of moving toward a safer church involves reaching a fuller understanding of the steps in an abused woman's journey. Another part involves no longer doing women more harm, either unknowingly or knowingly.

These can be difficult tasks for pastors and church leaders who are approached by women who've experienced trauma and abuse. Most seminaries require only one counseling class in their masters of divinity program. So many folks who are entrusted to lead our churches have not been adequately trained in how to sit with the broken, not to mention that they have zero training in how to work with complex PTSD and trauma victims. It's no wonder, then, given the lack of training and other resources, that many goodhearted pastors look for quick fixes to complicated issues or quick answers to complicated questions.

The Bible, however, has never been a place for quick fixes or answers. Theologian Peter Enns puts it this way in his book *The Bible Tells Me So*: "The Bible is not a Christian owner's manual but a story—a diverse story of God and how his people have connected with him over the centuries, in changing circumstances and situations."[7]

This is, arguably, something much better than a source of quick fixes. The Bible can be used as a part of the healing journey to enter more deeply into painful emotions. This is far more useful than the more common approach of *spiritual bypassing*, which is when spirituality is used to escape painful emotions rather than enter into them. Encouraging someone to engage in spiritual bypassing rather than genuine spiritual healing is a form of abuse. If you have suffered spiritual abuse, then you know exactly what I am talking about. Whether you know abuse personally or are a church leader using this book as a resource to become better equipped, it's important to come to understand more fully the complexity of abuse and the process of healing from it.

Here are a few practical steps pastors and leaders can take to help women to recover from abuse:

- *Acknowledge her experience.* For so much of her experience, she has been gaslit and minimized. What if you just start by saying that you believe her, that it is not her fault?

In doing so, you may be offering exactly the loving support she needs. You may also learn something new yet painful, but this discovery may be exactly what *you* need.

- *Don't try to fix her!* Just practice being a safe and loving presence. She needs to rage, vent, and grieve. She is trying to make sense of so much confusion about her relationship with her partner and with God. She needs a kind presence, not someone with answers and solutions. *Now, that being said, a large caveat here is that if she is in danger, she will need immediate help and answers. She doesn't merely need a kind presence if she is not safe at home. You need to be ready with resources to help her get safe.*

- *Understand that she is testing you.* This is not a negative—she has been hurt by so many well-intentioned men that she is counting the cost and making sure you are for real. She has heard good words and various promises time and time again; she is watching to see if you are different. Even if you believe her, she will still be experiencing a lot of feelings. She will still be angry for all the time that was lost when her husband was acting out and all she went through with him. As her pastor, be gentle. Remember that she is in recovery, learning how to walk again, learning how to live after the war. She will need your support as she relearns the dance of intimacy and repair.

- *If she needs to leave (i.e., separation, divorce, or leaving the church), let her do so without repercussions.* You can love her well by allowing her freedom. Previously, the church has grasped for control; now the church must surrender, although it will be terrifying. Church leadership can gain a new perspective and move into maturity and healing. First and foremost, she must feel safe. Her husband may have done too much damage for her to remain in the marriage. If she feels unsafe, it is because he broke his marriage vows (i.e., porn, abuse, being unfaithful, or harming her in other ways). In some cases, she might not be giving up on the marriage but actually fighting for it, fighting for new, genuine intimacy and love without the old dynamics of power, control, and insecurity. Nothing can be reborn without first dying. In addition, the husband might need to leave the home if she is asking for space. He has done damage, and he must embrace the consequences of his actions.

- *Resist the urge to be defensive.* A woman who feels triggered and is in full PTSD mode from abuse may lash out. She is having an intense reaction about her husband, about her experiences in the church. Pastors can show their care by not taking her anger personally. If the church has failed her, then humbly acknowledge your blind spots and do better. If you feel yourself becoming defensive, take time to figure out why. Don't project your reactions onto this wounded woman. Learn to dodge the hits with wisdom, calm, discipline, and maturity. Mastering this skill can help you love yourself and your traumatized congregants well.

Throughout human history, women have borne the brunt of the epidemic of male violence. Men, this is our work; we must have the courage to do the necessary work to become safe and kind. We can choose to be part of the solution, becoming allies rather than unintentional harmers of women. Leaders, let's normalize talking about issues of trauma and abuse so that we can more readily equip our churches to handle these evils.

It's Not Just Men

I have talked a lot about the impact of patriarchy, misogyny, and pornography in the church and about the impact of men who misuse their power, but what about women? What role have they played in keeping the damaging system in place? Why do many of them uphold something that hurts so many women so deeply?

Well, the answer is they have internalized those messages. Writer Aya Hibben defines *internalized misogyny* as "the sexist way women learn to view both themselves and other women."[8] It is taught—you guessed it—by men in positions of power and by other women who are part of the system, and "it's a subconscious way of degrading yourself and other women based on sexist ideas of how women should act, dress, or speak."[9]

Remember our review of commonly misapplied Scriptures and damning theologies that have been pedaled throughout Christendom? It makes sense that women would come to believe these degrading messages about their own goodness and worth. After all, that's what they've been told the Bible teaches.

But just as men can become better allies to women, women can become more informed, better equipped allies for themselves. Hibben continues by writing, "Recognizing our own internalized misogyny is essential to equality. Women must continue to support and empower each other, which is impossible without empowering ourselves first."[10]

Molly, from my study, shared her experience of another woman in the church who had internalized these crippling messages and attempted to convince her to comply with the male-dominated ministry world:

> The most egregious sexism was when a female leader tried to teach me to approach or speak manipulatively to some of the male pastors, trying to make them think my idea was their idea such that I could "get [my] way" rather than just discussing issues and coming to positive, group-serving, God-honoring conclusions like adults . . . that's how little value this culture places on female voices.

Rather than being a part of the solution, this female coworker was part of the problem. When she first encountered the idea that females needed to manipulate their male coworkers to be heard, she might have questioned or addressed it in some way. Instead, she went along with it and also trained other women to submit to a system that causes them much alienation and heartache.

Resolving this issue starts with men—men getting out of themselves and seeing the world through the lens of women—but they can't do it alone. It will take both men and women to overcome abuse and trauma issues within the church. And when we work together to become trauma- and abuse-informed, more of God's image bearers will thrive, and we will more clearly reflect God's glory to the world.

A Letter from a Pastor

Years ago, I got this message from a kindhearted pastor trying to learn how to navigate potential abuse allegations in his church.

Dear Andrew,

As a pastor, I'm wondering if I am prepared to handle potential sexual assault allegations in our church. I pray this never happens, but it seems the odds are not in my favor. My knee-jerk reaction would be to help the individual that has been victimized, assist them in contacting the police, and build a support system around them. Here is my question: We both know that people lie, and if I automatically side with the accuser/victim, then I could potentially unfairly accuse an innocent person. On the other hand, I would never want a true victim to feel like I was writing them off. I feel as though I should never question someone in that situation, but a woman falsely accused my pastor when I was younger. He was found to be innocent, and she admitted making it up, but his reputation was already tarnished by that point. So how do I proceed with caution, protecting the victim

but at the same time not jumping to the wrong conclusion?
Thanks for your time.

Here is how I responded.

Dear Pastor,

Thank you for your humble engagement with this difficult
topic. Your presence is desperately needed in this ongoing
conversation. You are right, the odds are not in your favor,
as one in three women will face some sexual or physical
violence in her life.

First, we must honor stories of victimization and take
them all very seriously. I would rather take these stories too
seriously than not seriously enough. Women do make false
claims, but statistics show that only 2–10 percent of alleged
victims make false accusations.[11] It is so very rare, but yes,
it does happen. What happens more often is that men are
perpetrators of rape against women (99 percent of rapes
are committed by men), and women are so traumatized
they forget what happened or block it out altogether. Far
too often, we turn a blind eye to those who are suffering
among us.

It is not up to you to determine whether the allegations
are true; let the law enforcement and the courts unravel that
side of things. Your role is to listen and honor both persons;
both the accuser and accused are image bearers of God and
deserve to be honored.

This men's club that is the evangelical church has to begin
to change its ways, or we will lose access to a part of God's
image—femininity. Thank you again for your question. My
hope is to link arms with you against the evil that is sexual
violence in this world.

Andrew J. Bauman[12]

We need more pastors like this one, aware and ready to engage their congregants in an authentic and humble way. If you are a pastor, you can start by following his example and by doing what I recommend in this book. Will you do the hard work to prepare yourself to engage in difficult conversations and complex issues without spiritual bypassing? Can you commit to living in the truth of whatever happens? False allegations do take place, but they are rare. Worse yet is when true allegations aren't treated with the seriousness they deserve. All allegations must be looked into and proper policies put in place. (We will review those policies in the final chapter.) But before we skip ahead to creating policies, we need to dive into some real-life examples of what the church's present-day engagement with women looks like and consider what we can learn from these stories.

EIGHT

The Church's Present-Day Engagement with Women

The truth about sexism in the church is that the church is not only a place where sexism is tolerated, it is actively harbored and justified.

Dr. Karoline M. Lewis, "The Truth about Sexism in the Church"

I began blogging nearly a decade ago about men's issues I was seeing in my private practice, mostly pornography and deceptive sexuality. I was using some of my own writings to help my clients (mostly men) because I could not find many helpful recovery materials for Christian men that were non-shaming, non-shallow, and trauma-informed. At the time, my author page had about eight hundred followers. Many women and betrayal-trauma recovery pages soon started sharing my posts and quotes. Wait. I thought I was writing to men. Why were so many women drawn to my material?

Since that time, my page has grown to have more than fifty-nine thousand followers, 80 percent of whom are women. I continue to write primarily to men, though I have learned much more about being on the other side of trauma and abuse. I have gained a better understanding of what women suffer regularly in our culture and churches. Although the twenty-first century has seen many advances in women's rights, church attendance among women has been in steady decline. There is no way to determine a single rationale for it, but one assumption is that as women have grown in strength and voice, they have begun to resist the church's historically poor engagement with women and have removed themselves from unhealthy congregations.[1]

Women are hungry to talk about the truth. They have felt gaslit and lied to by their partners and are desperate for men to be honest about their struggles and their internal emotional worlds. And too many men still refuse to listen to "emotional and illogical" women. Part of the reason I completed my study was to provide data to a wider audience that shows conclusively that when we talk about sexism and abuse in the church, we're not just "exaggerating" or "overreacting"; it's a real and widespread problem.

As I mentioned, I interviewed eight women in depth about their experiences working in the Protestant church; these interviewees were chosen randomly from the hundred-plus of my survey respondents who volunteered to engage further in my study. These women came from all over the country, and none attended the same church. All were Caucasian (which was definitely a limiting factor in my study) and ranged in age from midtwenties to midfifties.

All had left their abusive churches; some had returned to attending a healthy church and some had not. Many had moved on to successful careers post-ministry; two were single and without children, three had been divorced and remarried, three were married, and six were mothers. They were all middle class, though many had fought hard to get out of poverty and rebuild their life after their betrayal and abuse. All are referred to by pseudonyms in this book. To ensure ethics, trustworthiness, and solid research practices, this part of my study was approved by my university's internal review board.

I conducted the interviews via Zoom over a period of four months, then transcribed, coded, and analyzed them so that I could glean real data to help the church be a safer place. This chapter reveals and analyzes those findings, unpacking what women in the church today can offer and teach all of us.

I asked the following questions:

1. How long did you work/volunteer in the church?
2. Did you feel like your opportunities were limited because you were a woman? If yes, how?
3. Do you feel like sexism and abuse were part of your church experience? If yes, how were you personally impacted?
4. Did you ever face sexual harassment or sexual misconduct at your church?
5. What do you believe the biggest blind spots were for your church leadership to understand women's experiences?
6. If you were to offer suggestions for creating safer church environments, what would you suggest?
7. What would you tell your younger self who is just starting to work at the church?
8. What gives you hope in facing this epidemic in the church?
9. In closing, is there anything else you would like me to know or any stories you want to share about your experience with the church?

The analysis of the interview data yielded three main themes and eight subthemes, which were identified as recurring in at least five of the eight participants' interviews. The first main theme was sexism and abuse with the subthemes of exploitation, grooming, and retraumatizing the victim. The second main theme was leadership failure with one subtheme: failed abuse interventions. And the final main theme was healing with the four subthemes of

8.1 Table 1

THEMES	Presence of Themes across Participants							
	1	2	3	4	5	6	7	8
SEXISM AND ABUSE	Yes	Yes	Yes	Yes	Yes	Yes	Yes	Yes
Exploitation	Yes	Yes	Yes	Yes	No	Yes	Yes	Yes
Grooming	Yes	Yes	Yes	Yes	Yes	Yes	Yes	Yes
Retraumatizing the Victim	Yes	Yes	Yes	Yes	Yes	Yes	Yes	Yes
LEADERSHIP FAILURE	Yes	Yes	Yes	Yes	Yes	Yes	Yes	Yes
Failed Abuse Interventions	Yes	Yes	Yes	No	Yes	Yes	Yes	Yes
HEALING	Yes	Yes	Yes	Yes	Yes	Yes	Yes	Yes
Redemption	Yes	Yes	Yes	Yes	Yes	Yes	Yes	Yes
Abuse Intervention	Yes	Yes	Yes	Yes	Yes	Yes	Yes	Yes
Creating Safety	Yes	Yes	Yes	Yes	Yes	Yes	Yes	Yes
Representation and Diversity	Yes	Yes	Yes	Yes	Yes	Yes	Yes	Yes

redemption, abuse intervention, creating safety, and representation and diversity. Table 1 lists these main themes and subthemes and the presence of each theme across the eight participants. If you need hard data to wrap your mind around the scope and severity of the problem in our churches, the rest of this chapter is for you.

Sexism and Abuse

One of the women I interviewed, Rebecca, said she and her sisters were forced by their parents to wear wetsuit-style bathing suits, called modesty swimsuits, when they went swimming. Rebecca's covered her entire torso to her neck. She said one of her father's friends commented that he was "thankful [he] could go swimming with [his] family because [he] did not have to worry about lusting because of how the girls dressed."

Likewise, Alison noted, "There were a couple of instances where pastoral staff members would make inappropriate comments about physical appearance . . . and then laugh it off. . . . I had one guy say, 'What? Is it wrong to appreciate God's creation?'"

She added that a youth pastor told her, "I'm a shoulders guy, so I'm going to need you to tell them to stop wearing sleeveless stuff." These comments from family, friends, and church leaders negatively impacted both Rebecca and Alison in how they viewed their self-worth and their relationship to their bodies. They began to heal from this sexism and abuse after years of their own therapy and being in relationship with healthy men who did not objectify their bodies but honored them.

Scenarios like these were common for participants who grew up in the Protestant church. Both Rebecca and Alison found themselves on the receiving end of sexism (which, as we defined earlier, is prejudice, stereotyping, or discrimination because of one's sex[2]). They were discriminated against merely because they had female bodies and seemingly caused arousal in the men around them. These male leaders then put the burden of their sexual arousal onto the women rather than dealing with their own relationship to it.

Many women surveyed felt discriminated against because of their sex and judged because of their bodies and clothes. Many had to fight off sexist remarks from leaders. All participants identified the theme of leadership failure in their experience of working in the Protestant church.

Rebecca's and Alison's stories are just two of many examples of an excessive leadership focus on women's clothing and so-called modesty. Rose shared her belief that the church placed the responsibility on women "for having bodies rather than holding men accountable for perverse thoughts." Numerous participants admitted they felt "shamed" for having a female body and that an "unfair responsibility" was imposed upon them by men in church leadership positions. Similarly, Kelley said she was made to wear dresses at church, and "I have a big butt, so I would always wear huge skirts to cover my butt because I didn't want men to lust after me."

Beth was also criticized for her choice of clothing. "Women could not wear tank tops. . . . It was like nine thousand degrees in this little country bumpkin church, and they [said], 'She cannot be on stage. She has a sleeveless shirt on.'" This shared experience of criticism for how one dresses is a form of discrimination and completely unfair to women, who were made to bear the responsibility for male arousal.

All eight interviewees shared stories of varying degrees of sexism in the Protestant church. The difference in rules and expectations for women was a common thread in participants' stories. As a young girl, Beth went to a church that was "very strict" about women not holding leadership positions. This caused a lot of self-doubt and a longing to not be a woman. She said she quickly learned she did not want to instruct children. "And I did not want to host tea parties. . . . I have memories of being a young girl, and I would sit in front of the mirror, and I would practice preaching." Years later, she went to work for a church in a leadership position, but as the church held to a belief that women could not be pastors, she could not hold the title of "pastor" even though she did the same work as her male colleagues. She described her leadership training through the church as attending classes until she became physically ill because of the disparity she perceived. "There [was] absolutely nothing different between what I was learning and my male colleagues, but at the completion of the training the men got [the title of] Reverend and women got [the title of] Consecrated Woman of Ministry."

When the male leader of the worship team got sick at Rose's church, the team planned for her to lead in his absence. She reported, "I had a beautiful set of music that I had worked hard on and was totally prepared for live music. And I have fifteen years of training in piano." However, church leaders told her that they were planning to play YouTube music videos and have an octogenarian male associate pastor lead instead. Rose's skills and abilities were deemed less important than having a male leader.

Theologian Karoline M. Lewis states, "Sexism in the church lives and thrives because it can ground its reasons for uncritical acquiescence to sexism on biblical and theological bases, without even having to work particularly hard."[3] The findings of my study bear this out. For example, Kelley indicated, "I heard all kinds of things: that women should submit to their husbands, that the husband is the head of the home, that women should not talk in church, [and] women should wear certain clothing." She was told "women should not speak up and not be disrespectful to their husbands." She also said these messages were taught as theological and biblical truth because "women are more easily deceived because of Eve, so women shouldn't be leaders in the church."

When Terry worked for the church as a women's ministry leader, the elders quickly dismissed her ideas when it came to church functions or community outreach ideas. She believed if she were a man, her opinions would have been valued more highly.

Libby said she got pregnant when she was eighteen years old and was forced to write a letter to the church and stand in front of the congregation and apologize. Yet the same was not required of the boy who impregnated her.

As mentioned earlier, abuse advocate and author Sarah McDugal defines spiritual abuse as "the misuse of theology, scripture, church position, or spiritual influence to control, cause harm to, exploit, or reduce the personhood of another."[4] I can't think of another type of abuse that more violates the soul of a person than spiritual abuse—to use God as a weapon of control rather than view God as the loving Spirit who gave us Jesus to die on the cross.

McDugal asserts that spiritual abuse can include actions such as using Scripture to avoid accountability, applying spiritual beliefs to gain an advantage, and leveraging spiritual leaders against someone.[5] Bible verses are misused to silence women, and women are convinced of their need to be taught more about God by men who indicate they are acting as the Holy Spirit on their behalf. Some church leaders also excuse destructive patterns or behaviors in the name of God.[6]

As participants shared their stories, similar themes unfolded. Each woman was subject to a series of affronts that included various sexual, psychological, emotional, and spiritual abuses. Anne experienced both blatant and subversive abuse while working at her church. "The abuse from my first husband was swept under the rug. It was not dealt with properly." Another woman shared about catching her husband using pornography and lying about it; after going to their pastor, he assured her that "every man struggles with it" and that she should be his accountability partner and "serve" him more (code for "offer him more sex") to help him with his struggles.

Libby experienced verbal abuse when a deacon yelled at her because her daughter was sitting next to a boy. "I've never even [been] talked to like this in my life." Even the language used by church leadership and the way it was delivered indicated a lack of respect for women.

Sexism and abuse can take many forms in the church, and my study results surfaced three common subthemes related to both: exploitation, grooming, and retraumatizing the victim.

Exploitation

Philosopher and ethics professor Dr. Matt Zwolinski defines *exploitation* as taking unfair advantage of someone's weaknesses or vulnerabilities.[7] Alison felt exploited by her church when she was asked to take over the girls' ministry. "I already had a [small] high school girl's group. . . . And that turned into the full responsibilities of a youth pastor [with] none of the support." Alison did not get a title, pay, or support from the church leadership but was exploited for her unpaid work with young girls in the youth group. Similarly, Kelley shared, "I was never paid to do the work I did. And I helped my husband plan Vacation Bible School, fall festival, [and] summer camps. I spent most of my free time volunteering." She left the job feeling underappreciated and taken advantage of.

Rose shared her story of feeling exploited by two different youth pastors for being a single woman "of marriage age." She reported that they said, "they wished I would date their sons. It was never about me or what I could do. The first one said, 'I wish you'd date my son and help him be the leader God wants him to be.'" The other youth pastor pressured her to sign a marriage contract to wed his son. "These are both youth leaders, and it was all about me serving their sons through my giftings." Rose did not feel valued for who she was but rather for what she could do for the pastors and their own personal agendas.

Jackie believed she was financially exploited by her church. When a church leader heard that she had received a twenty-seven-thousand dollar settlement, he approached her and asked for a gift for the pastor. She ended up giving five thousand dollars toward the pastor's bonus, then used her remaining money to pay for school expenses. After a year, Jackie had no money left and became homeless. She explained, "And the church was like, 'Well, make sure that you keep coming to volunteer.'" The church did not offer to assist Jackie with housing or financial support in her time of great need, even though they knew what a difficult situation she was in. She felt exploited and abandoned. "And so, I was like, that five thousand dollars sure would be nice about now to find myself a place to live." When Jackie had money, she was considered valuable to her church. Once her fortunes changed, the tables turned. The church expected her to tithe and to continue to volunteer her time, but they didn't assume any responsibility for helping her when she needed financial help.

These stories of exploitation were similar for seven out of eight participants. Rose's church had taught her that her worth and purpose were only in being a wife and a mother, and so she worried greatly when she had trouble getting pregnant. She said, "My entire existence as a woman was about being a wife and a mom." She believed her in-laws regretted their son had married her because of her struggles with infertility, and she thought, *Ugh, these other guys that might have liked me sure dodged a bullet by not marrying me, because I might not be able to have kids.*

Grooming

Libby was conditioned from an early age to believe females were destined for specific domestic roles. "I was the cooker, the cleaner, the laundry, all of that, while my brother didn't necessarily have to help." She was taught certain standards and expectations for masculinity and femininity. She said many women in the church have been taught not to trust their intuition, adding, "The church does an excellent job at teaching women subtly how to reject themselves as a whole."

Libby's story reflects another theme of sexism and abuse that arose from the interviews: a set of behaviors and actions known as *grooming*. Authors Susan Raine and Stephen A. Kent assert that even though there is scant research on grooming specifically within religious contexts, some understandings and definitions do exist.[8] As mentioned earlier, grooming involves being made vulnerable for future abuse. It is often referred to in the context of child abuse, although grooming can happen at any age. Specific goals of perpetrators include gaining access to the victim, gaining the victim's compliance, and maintaining the victim's secrecy to avoid disclosure. This trust is built over time and can strengthen an offender's access to abuse. They may use the excuse, "Look at all I have done for you" to justify their behavior.[9] Put simply, grooming is about gaining someone's trust in a way that makes the person vulnerable to harm.

Sometimes that harm is sexual in nature. Jackie was raped by a spiritual leader who taught her science class in a homeschool co-op. She recalled, "One of the dads taught [the] science class and used that position to groom me. His family was asked to leave another church because of his inappropriate advances on a young woman there. So, they came to our church, and leadership was warned about him, and they did nothing."

Furthermore, Jackie was encouraged to keep silent about the details for over a decade so as not to damage the church's reputation. "The pastor would not call it rape. He called it nonconsensual sex, which is just an absolute joke," she commented. In this situation, Jackie felt not only misunderstood but also dismissed by her pastor.

She also noted how close she'd felt to her betrayer. "He was a person I trusted. I thought if anything happened to my parents, he and his wife would raise me." Grooming and building trust are common tactics for those looking to perpetrate abuse in the church, according to participants.

Author Anna Salter shares a quote from a former youth pastor who abused approximately a hundred boys before he was caught: "I considered church people easy to fool . . . they have a trust that comes from being Christians . . . they seem to want to believe in the good that exists in all people. . . . I think they want to believe in people. And because of that, you can easily convince, with or without convincing words."[10]

If you're still not convinced that churches must proactively implement programs and policies to prevent sexism and abuse, create safeguards, and improve training, read that quote again. (I will address policies and programs that can help create these safeguards in the final chapter of this book, "Steps toward Creating a Safe Church.")

It's important to note that not all grooming is sexual, however. Sometimes it involves conditioning a person to believe they are inferior. This type of grooming usually falls under the category of sexism rather than abuse (though it may well leave women more vulnerable to abuse). Rose said, "You did not see the abuse because it was very subtle and built into you through the years. It was physically a part of you and became a source of your identity."

Terry summarized what she was taught: "Men are in charge, so get in line." Similarly, Libby said men "have been taught that [women are] weak and that men don't have to step up to the plate."

Libby had been taught to believe that women were created to serve men and thus suppressed many of her own goals and desires. These messages can demoralize women, misinform their relationship with their own bodies, and, in many ways, retraumatize them in a place where safety is often assumed.

Retraumatizing the Victim

Terry reported about her experience with some of the church leaders while she was on staff but going through a painful divorce: "I was trying to get divorced from someone who was emotionally, verbally, and spiritually abusive who also was a deacon in the church at the time. They kept trying to get me to meet with my abuser, trying to force reconciliation." She added, "The treatment I was getting from the men at church was retraumatizing."

Retraumatization is defined as "one's reaction to a traumatic exposure that is colored, intensified, amplified, or shaped by one's reactions and adaptational style to previous traumatic experiences."[11] Professor and clinical psychologist Dr. Pam C. Alexander explains how a later event or incident can bring up feelings—even physical sensations in the body—that are rooted in the original trauma: "Although the exposure may not be inherently traumatic but may only carry reminders of the original traumatic event or relationship, retraumatization typically refers to the reemergence of symptoms previously experienced as a result of the trauma."[12]

Participants shared many stories about their experiences while working at churches that were retraumatizing to their healing journey. These included being ostracized by that very community. Kelley recalled her feelings of being retraumatized after her divorce from her abusive husband who, like Terry's husband, was a deacon in their church. She stated, "These church people, I would bring them meals after they had babies and be at their family's funerals and rub their feet when they were in the hospital. And . . . everyone [turned] their back on me except for one family. I had to rebuild my whole social sphere. I had to find a new support system."

Rallying around the person who has been harmed would be the most loving decision, but many times the opposite happens, perpetrating deeper pain. Kelley needed support, yet her husband was the one left in good standing with her church community. The public image he put forth was so different from the emotional and spiritual abuse he perpetrated against Kelley.

Similarly, Jackie was retraumatized when she was forced to apologize to her rapist's wife and daughter. She said the church leadership "made me make a formal apology to [my abuser's] wife less than twenty-four hours after they got me away from him and then his daughter the next day." Jackie was in her late teens, and her abuser was in his forties and had been her teacher and spiritual leader. She added that the church leadership said that both parties were wrong and that she, the victim, was "a tempter." In addition, as a way to make her "clean" again, Jackie shared, "My mother wanted me to cut my hair because my hair belonged to my [future] husband, and she prayed over me and declared me a re-virgin."

Another retraumatizing theme for participants was the promotion of a "marriage no matter what" ideology we discussed earlier. Again, this idea centers on the concept that a marriage covenant is more important than the safety (in all ways) of each partner.

These stories of church leaders trying to get participants to reconcile with their abusive husbands are also examples of the next main theme of my study results: systemic leadership failure.

Leadership Failure

When Alison told the pastoral counselor at her church about physical abuse by her husband, he looked at her then-husband, who flat-out denied the abuse. This counselor, who had "no counseling certifications," then dismissed her reports by telling her, "We carry our cross and our burdens. And the Lord never told us that it would be easy." Not taking Alison's claims of abuse seriously left her vulnerable to more harm and abuse.

Alison viewed her church's response as a failure of leadership to protect her. But what kind of leadership would have been needed to create a different result? Healthy or ethical leadership refers to "the demonstration of normative appropriate conduct through personal actions and interpersonal relationships, and the promotion of such conduct to followers through two-way communication, reinforcement, and decision-making."[13] Understanding what healthy, effective leadership involves is crucial; this theme of leadership failure was present in all eight participants' interviews.

Jackie said years after her sexual abuse by the father in her homeschool co-op, the church leadership admitted, "We did not know what we were supposed to do. How are we supposed to know? We weren't experts." Jackie implored, "You were supposed to know that you weren't experts and that you needed somebody who was an expert." She stated that the pastor managed her abuse claims, and it went "horribly wrong because he did not have the proper training or abuse awareness to lead effectively." It should go without saying that proper training for all leaders in the church is important. (I highly recommend this course from my mentor, Dr. Nancy Murphy: *Speaking Up! Recognizing and Addressing Domestic Violence in the Christian Community*.)

Failure of church leadership can take many forms, including sexual engagement and, perhaps more commonly, excessive attempts to avoid the appearance of such engagement. Many men in church leadership positions fail to lead their congregations well and have been enmeshed in scandal.[14] One reactionary response to that phenomenon has many pastors avoiding contact with women in their ministry. Rose shared, "One elder at our church said, 'If I ever have an issue with you, I will, of course, go to your husband.'" In responding to her confusion, he added, "I just want to be above reproach. I just don't want that to be read into." Rose felt disrespected because the elder required her husband to be present during certain conversations. In another example of leadership failure, Kelley asserted that she was taught, "Pastors should not have one-on-one counseling in an office with a woman because it could lead to something." She argued church leaders "have outward appearances of righteousness but [are] just not living it in the real world." During her time attending that specific church, that same pastor was sexually harassing her via inappropriate text messages and regular comments about her physical appearance.

The leaders in these examples held positions of authority but weren't really leading. Pastor and writer Vanessa Stricker queries, "Shouldn't we be following leaders who look like Jesus, leaders who don't grasp for worldly power but understand that their authority comes from the Spirit?"[15] As author Lee Colan points out, Jesus demonstrated a model of leadership that was based on having a character of integrity and a posture of servanthood, being a great storyteller, and leading with strong conviction and compassion.[16] It should go without saying that those who have experienced abuse need to be listened to and cared for, not dismissed, blamed, ignored, or marginalized.

Libby believed the church could be the "most unwelcoming, hypocritical organization ever, and full of judgment." Jackie suggested leaders and congregants should "see the world through the eyes of Jesus," stating, "we have to be able to see through power and oppression instead of letting that lens obscure our view of the way things really are."

The data collected from my interviews is clear and is supported by review of the ample literature on the subject: leadership failures only continue when systemic issues are not addressed. Ultimately, these leadership failures in the church are best addressed when the pastor is not the sole decision maker but has a team capable of providing accountability and ensuring follow-through. Healthy, diverse leadership teams have checks and balances in place so one person cannot abuse their position and power.

In my interviews, one subtheme related to leadership failures was reported: seven out of eight participants experienced failed abuse interventions. Let's take a look.

Failed Abuse Interventions

Jackie said church leadership investigated her story of abuse but then failed to contact the authorities. She shared, "They did this whole investigation, and it didn't make any sense because their investigation revealed that he did rape me and a crime or multiple crimes were committed, but they never tried to do anything with that information." This is a painful example of one type of leadership failure.

In his foreword to author and trauma expert Peter A. Levine's book *In an Unspoken Voice*, Dr. Gabor Maté states, "Trauma is not what happens to us, but what we hold inside in the absence of an empathetic witness."[17] Having such a witness with "credibility, empathy, and capacity for prevention"[18] might have led to different results in the following examples of misguided attempts or complete failures to intervene. Often these stories reveal an absence of sufficient empathy to move the witnesses to take action. Many of these experiences left participants feeling even more alone and distraught.

Jackie's story is particularly poignant. She believed the church failed to protect her because they did not contact the proper authorities and her abuser faced no consequences. Jackie thought the abuse intervention was helpful at first because at least she was able to talk more openly about what happened, but by the time intervention ended, it had become more harmful to her well-being because of how little those who worked with her actually understood about the psychological impact of sexual abuse. Their advice to read more Scripture and work on forgiving her abuser was damaging and confusing.

This problem is probably representative of the church as a whole; of course, not all churches are this unaware and unhealthy, but far too many women report similar stories.

Healing

"The word *healing* comes from the old-English term *haelen*, meaning 'wholeness' and often refers to the process of moving toward a desired wholeness or achievement of cohesion."[19] Many participants had difficult and painful experiences while working in the Protestant church, yet their painful experiences did not stop them from pursuing healing. Kelley's experience of healing came through difficult but much-needed hard work to move beyond the abuse. She shared,

> I have been in therapy, and I have fought my own demons and just realized I can do it. I can pull myself up with my bootstraps and can support myself and my kids without [my ex-husband], no matter what he tries to do. He tried every way to financially abuse me. It is just getting up every day and doing what I need to do and taking care of my kids. You do not know how strong you are until you must be.

Beth's mentor told her, "You'll know it's time to leave when staying requires that you compromise the integrity of who you are." She proffered this advice to help Beth understand it was time to step down from her ministry position. As participants navigated their negative experiences, some admitted they used it as inspiration to seek out that wholeness and cohesion within themselves.

Sometimes women find that in order to achieve this healing, they must leave their church. Rose said she "wished she could tell [her] younger self to leave her church and reevaluate her own self-worth. I had no self-worth. And my whole identity [as] a home-schooled Baptist girl was to find a husband and be a good godly wife and mom." She added she would tell her younger self that "those are wonderful, noble things in the right context and with the right person. [My] relationship with God is not dependent on if [I] can land a Christian husband and have babies. There is more to having a nurturing personality than being able to have children."

Rose said that the messages about marriage kept her further "imprisoned" to men and their ideals and beliefs rather than allowing her to form her own. Healing for Rose looked like deconstructing these damaging messages about her worth being tied to marriage and having children and finding her worth in being an image bearer of God.

Terry shared part of her healing from all the wounds she suffered while working in a male-dominated church has been in seeing men step up and use their positions of power to elevate women's voices and advocate for equality.

> It gives me a lot of hope to see a male speaking out on it, but it is much rarer. I would tell the other ministers, "This is never going to change until men start speaking out about it because women don't have a voice. The only people who can give us a voice are the men because they are in a powerful position. Until you're willing to take that step and be the advocate, it's not going to happen."

How many other women need to experience men speaking up and advocating for the marginalized and silenced?

Redemption

In one form or another, the theme of redemption came up in my interviews with all eight participants. After experiencing failures from their church leaders and while engaging in their own healing process, many (though not all) participants used their experiences to help others who were undergoing similar oppression.

Terry said she was working with victims of domestic violence and sought to use her pain to help others heal from sexism and abuse in the Protestant church. Other participants expressed they had yet to heal from the pain they suffered from religious leaders. Some mentioned attending ongoing therapy sessions.

The need for healing should go without saying. Dr. Diane Langberg states,

> Victims experience depression, anxiety, posttraumatic stress disorder, substance abuse, self-injury, alienation, sleep disturbance,

distorted thinking (I am evil; I am trash; it is my fault), and loss of faith. Studies have documented that when the abuser is a leader in the faith community, the damage is particularly pronounced.[20]

Many of the women in this study experienced those things. They also found inside themselves a source of wisdom that pointed them toward healing and often went the further step of self-assigning a leadership role to try to end cycles of abuse.

Terry said if she could speak to her younger self, she would say, "Find a faith denomination that allows you to be fully who God created you to be and doesn't put you in this hierarchical order because you were born a female." Beth said, "I will trailblaze. I will mother a movement." She believed she could continue to break through the "stained-glass ceiling," as Professor Peter Feuerherd states, and continue to blaze a new trail for other women in ministry.[21] Regarding redemption from pain inflicted by sexism and abuse, Jackie stated, "The church tried to destroy me and a lot of other people, and I'm picking up the pieces with myself and trying to help other people. I am trying really hard to teach and encourage leaders."

Psychologist and leading sex abuse expert Dr. Dan Allender has shared his own experience of trauma and redemption. "Sexual abuse has affected for good and ill everything I have done and will do on this earth. The harm from the past simply does not go away."[22] He compares his experience of sexual abuse to another trauma: a car accident in which he was severely injured. "I cannot imagine what my condition would be without the immense care I have received, but even more so I cannot allow myself to consider what my life would be like if that accident had never occurred."[23] He argues that sexual abuse is similar in that one can never "fully eradicate the consequences of the harm" yet proffers he also has an opportunity to use the experience for transformation and redemption, unlike the car accident. "Would I trade these benefits for not being harmed? Of course, without a doubt; I would do so in an instant. But that is not an option. . . . It is best to embrace heartache and determine to use it for larger purposes."[24] Allender asserts that finding purpose and meaning within the suffering does not justify it, but there can be learning gained despite it.

Rose said her sister told her, "Maybe the ordinariness of your story would speak to women exactly like you who aren't in these extreme situations and don't see the abuse." Thus, Rose thought she could use her life experience to help other women who were also possibly dismissing harm and help free them from abuse.

Terry also said that though she would never wish for the harm she experienced, she has found purpose in it by helping other women with similar experiences through domestic violence recovery. But she knows she can't do this work alone and needs more male allyship. She also stated that she feels hope as more and more men speak out against abuse. Helping women in violent relationships get out and get safe is part of her redemption story, but seeing men step up and use their power for good rather than evil will help Terry fully heal.

Jackie has "tried to encourage and teach leaders [about abuse]. I am picking up the pieces and trying to help other people." Similarly, Anne shared, "I want to be an advocate. I want to support [others]. I think [abuse] needs to be called out because it is rampant." Anne sought to advocate for other abused women. She, Jackie, and other participants have not let abuse limit who they become. In fact, they've used their experiences to reach out and help others.

I received a lot of wisdom from the interviewees on the topic of redemption. Their comments touched upon the other subthemes of healing: abuse intervention, creating safety (for both individuals and churches), and representation and diversity.

Abuse Intervention

For many women, redeeming their experiences of sexism and abuse involves joining a community where abuse intervention is a high priority. Others speak up in the churches they already attend. Some women participate in interventions themselves. Others find it redemptive simply to be a part of a community where such actions are prioritized and valued.

Anne noted the importance of congregants having input rather than just top-down leadership directives. Regarding her new church experience, she said, "Everyone is encouraged to be a part of and share their thoughts, which I think is huge. Everyone has a voice, including all the women." This important part of Anne's new church experience has helped her cultivate safety in her community.

Kelley added that educating church leaders on issues of domestic abuse is vital for abuse intervention. She recognized the importance of continued training in fostering a safe church environment after her horrific experience taught her how little her church leaders understood what she went through. Similarly, Jackie shared the significance of relaying her story of abuse openly years later in the same church setting where her abuses occurred.

> When I told my story, another woman realized how bad her experience was and shared it with me. The following week, she shared it with the whole group. And then more people started sharing— people I have known my entire life. None of them had ever talked about it, and we found that half of the people in the group had some [similar] personal experience.

Jackie also believed she was helping intervene in abuse by fostering an environment of openness and authenticity that helped women feel seen, known, and accepted.

Many women have myriad responsibilities besides employment, such as family and community commitments, which could also be a contributing factor in declining church attendance.[25] In 2015, Barna found that 33 percent of women think it's very important to attend a local church while 27 percent of women do not think it's important to attend church at all.[26] In Christian ministry, this is a reality for many women; however, church leaders can become allies to help change women's negative experiences in the church.[27]

Creating Safety

All eight participants commented about what creating safety within the church meant for them. It is the work of church leadership to make sure they are creating safe environments and not being complicit with sexism and abuse. Dr. Diane Langberg describes the challenging work of self-reflection and removing deception in church leadership to provide safety in congregations:

> Our failure to see and do these things is, in part, an exposure of our extremely limited grasp of the nature of sin and its tentacles in our own lives. We would not be complicit with abuse wherever we find it if this were not so. Repentance is hard. It means a complete change of our thought processes, our impulses, and our choices, little by little. . . . It is not simply stopping a behavior. It is not words and tears. It is a slow undoing of deceptions—deceptions that allow us to feel okay about ourselves.[28]

Beth described feeling "seen" on her first day of working at a new, healthier church, stating, "I sat down and had a youth pastor and a pastor of a local church [tell me] they wanted to affirm my call to ministry. And I remember I sat there crying like, 'I can't believe a man is saying this to me.'" She also shared what it felt like to have a male pastor support her in her ministry position. "Every time he would be like, 'I love you. I am proud of you. Excellent job. You can do this.' He was so kind, saying, 'As often as your brain and body need to recalibrate that you're safe in this space, I'll give that to you.'" Beth believes this is what good leadership and creating safety look like for women who have suffered sexism and abuse in the church.

Anne spoke about the safety of her current church. "There's a lot of input from all members. Meetings are incredibly open.

Everyone is encouraged to be a part and share their thoughts and their voice." The thought that all members of the church congregation had input was healing for her after previously being ignored.

What does a church that does not prioritize creating safety look like? Beth shared how, when she was on the church staff, a female congregant felt she needed to set safeguards and boundaries for her husband because she didn't want to get raped, and in response the male church leadership said she was "emotionally abusing him." Church leaders must be better trained in understanding abuse dynamics and issues of power and control, or these situations can become quite dangerous.

Kelley talked about the importance of abuse recognition training in creating safe churches. She said, "Domestic abuse training is huge because it's more likely for abusive men to be attracted to churches that have patriarchal, misogynistic messages that are covertly used from Bible verses that are misinterpreted." Kelley believed this type of abuse awareness training would be helpful for both staff and congregants to help create safer church environments for women. (Such training is available through organizations such as Called to Peace Ministries, Northwest Family Life, Psalm 82 Ministry, and GRACE.)

Though churches have a responsibility to create safety, as we've seen, sometimes they don't. Either way, individuals within and without the church are also called to do what they can to make safe spaces for others and for themselves. Rose said, "My friend circle is smaller [now], but it is better, and it is safer." She also said she left her church and started taking anxiety medication, as did other participants. "I have been learning to be brave even if I am scared," she added. "It is not easy and at times terrifying but at times needed." Participants said they did what was needed to feel safe and to create a new life after abuse.

Alison noted that another way to create safety is by making amends. She remembers unwillingly and unknowingly supporting a harmful system.

During my whole deconstruction and reconstruction journey over the last three years, I have reconnected with a lot of my former students and sat down with them and said, "I must apologize to you. I was doing what I thought I was supposed to do, and I was saying what I thought I was supposed to say, but it was wrong. And so, if any of the things that I have taught you have caused you any personal harm or have damaged you in any way, I want to talk about that and make amends because I was wrong. There was nothing wrong with you."

For Alison, this was an example of acknowledging her mistakes and creating safety for those she led. Church leaders could benefit by following her great example.

Representation and Diversity

Church leadership that's made up solely of white men does more than just subtly communicate that white men matter more than anyone else. It also shuts out the voices of people who represent the breadth and range of the congregation. Such leaders suffer from narrow vision that blinds them to the experiences of other people.

Professor and author Trevin Wax asserts, "The more voices we have access to, the bigger our Bible gets—the more we see what is there, behind our cultural blinders."[29] Diverse lived experiences can increase understanding of the biblical text. Diverse representation in church leadership is important.[30] Each participant in the study spoke about the importance of representation and diversity in the makeup of the church and its leadership, and many spoke about how greater diversity in leadership, had it been present, may have protected them from harm.

Rose spoke about the importance of women in leadership and creating representation in which a younger generation of girls may "see themselves." She stated, "Call women in to teach when you see teenage girls that are gifted in leadership. Do not ask them who they are going to marry." Rose believes this type of representation could have helped her by making her not feel so alone and may make a difference in the next generation of young leaders growing up in the church. She hopes that "they know the power of their own voices" and will be more honored and appreciated in Protestant church culture.

Terry shared, "If your leadership doesn't reflect the same demographics as your membership, then [the] part of your membership that's not represented in your leadership is not going to be heard, whether it's females, people of color, [or] other marginalized groups." Similarly, Kelley shared, "Having women as part of the leadership, I think, is important. Women have a viewpoint that men just do not see and cannot understand."

This theme of representation was present in all eight participant's interviews, and all noted the importance of having women as a part of the church leadership team.

What Does All This Mean?

There are numerous implications from this research regarding the effects of sexism and abuse. Many participants in the study have suffered lasting psychological effects of sexism and abuse. Many indicated they suffered from severe anxiety and depression because of their experiences in the Protestant church. Others have expressed a distrust of men. Rebecca said, "I am still in therapy and likely will be for life as a result of my past trauma in the church."

Alison said she had blocked out the trauma until the last three years of her therapy, which brought to the surface the painful memory of the church leaders' dismissal of her husband's physical abuse of her and being told to "carry her cross." Rose said she "had a purity ring and was told to save her first kiss for marriage." Thus, at the age of twelve, she made a commitment not to have sex and not to kiss before marriage. She believed the constant rules and pressure to live up to this led her to have an anxiety disorder.

Sexism and abuse can also break down relationships within families and cause further isolation and distance that are a struggle to overcome. Jackie shared, "I'm not talking currently with my parents because my dad said that I'm trying to destroy the church." When Jackie began to tell the story of her sexual abuse by an older leader in the church, her own family and elders in the church felt threatened. This is the opposite of what she needed from them and not the posture of a loving and safe family or church. As Langberg states,

> No system—family, church, community or institution—is truly God's work unless it is full of truth and love. Toleration of sin, pretense, disease, crookedness or deviation from the truth means the system is in fact not the work of God, no matter the words used to describe it. I fear we have a tendency as humans to submit ourselves to some command or idea of men, of the past, of tradition, of a systemic culture and in so doing, refuse to listen to and obey the living and ever-present God.[31]

Jackie shared the fallout and estrangement she experienced after she told her parents about the abuse. "My parents kicked me out. I was homeless, living out of my car." She was penalized for telling her story, which helped foster the toxic environment where sexism and abuse flourished.

A related implication is the church's reputation and, thereby, its ability to attract and retain members. Thanks, in part, to the rise of #MeToo, there is heightened attention on women who experience abuse. The #MeToo movement was founded by activist Tarana Burke in 2006, but it really gained traction in 2017 when actor Alyssa Milano asked people to share their own experiences of sexual assault and sexual harassment on social media with #MeToo.[32] Since the movement began, women have more commonly sought help, named their abusers publicly, and proceeded with litigation.[33] This has included abusers within the church, often tagged as #ChurchToo.

During church scandals, many congregants and potential congregants can become cynical about and distrust the church. Given the church's track record of moral failings, this is understandable. Yet, because of this, even fewer people feel comfortable within the church's walls, and the Christian community has lost credibility and become a less trustworthy place for the most vulnerable in society.

This research confirms that women in the church today are hurting deeply because of their mistreatment and subordination. They long to be seen and have their voices not only heard but reckoned with. When women are treated as equals in advancing the kingdom of God, we all flourish. I am reminded of the scriptural truth of the *imago dei*, which states how all humankind—both men and women—bear God's image (Gen. 1:27). When men and women live and work together to bring God's presence to earth, we can release the fullness of God.

As we've seen, women are working under sometimes terrible circumstances to bring about change. Men need to do their part too. Let's look at some of the challenges men face and what often keeps them from helping to create the safe churches women deserve and need.

NINE

Speaking Man to Man

Some of the proudest moments in the history of this country are grounded in the principle that members of dominant groups have a critical role to play in the struggle for equality.

Jackson Katz, *The Macho Paradox*

No one would have said it out loud, but in the white, evangelical, southern utopia where I grew up, we all knew it was true: men ruled the world. My presidents were always men. My pastors were always men. Most CEOs, elected officials, and anyone I knew with real power, authority, or influence were, like me, male. I wanted power too. Not simply for power's sake; I genuinely wanted to make a difference in the world—and I thought that developing a dominant masculinity was the answer.

This orientation to male power also shaped the way I interpreted Scripture while I was getting my undergraduate degree in Bible and religion. All my theological understanding had a tinge of sexism (I just didn't know it yet), making me, as a male, feel better about myself and somehow more important. Women were meant to play a subservient or complementary role in the church; after all, I reasoned, wasn't that simply God's designed order?

But viewing the world through this lens isn't a neutral act. Eventually, it affects the way we interact with others. It certainly did for me. When I got my first job out of college as a youth and college pastor, my sexist views of Scripture and of God unfortunately led me to abuse my position of power.

Let me clarify what I mean. I wasn't blatantly abusive—and despite attention-grabbing headlines, most pastors aren't. Most of my choices regarding my mistaken thoughts were more insidious than overt. My abuse consisted mostly of misinterpretation and misapplication of a few biblical passages to put women in their so-called rightful place. I never intended to be abusive when I got into ministry, but that is what I became. Most of the time during my decade of serving, I remained blissfully unaware of how more than half of the church—women—potentially experienced my sexist teachings and behavior. I truly wanted to help the hurting, love people, and show others God's love.

And so, the elevation of men in my mind continued to take shape, unchallenged. In the church where I served nearly twenty years ago, the entire pastoral team (except the children's ministry, of course) was led by men, and our goal was to cater to men's needs first to win the men over. After all, men were the heads of households, weren't they? So our collective thought was if the men became excited about our church, then they would ultimately lead their families to the Lord, a trickle-down spirituality of sorts. We had gatherings for men and events designed to make men feel more comfortable: hunting, fishing, golf tournaments, basketball games, cookouts, a bow and arrow night (yes, really), car shows—whatever stereotypical male activities we could do to get men in the door. The patriarchy was in the water, and we were all drinking from the fountain without even realizing that it was poisoned and we were getting sick.

Besides being surrounded only by people who looked and thought like me, I bolstered my abusive behavior with my secret pornography use. Pornography mixed with a misapplied doctrine helped teach me that women were created for my enjoyment, and they were meant to serve me and my male counterparts.

Today, I can clearly see how my skewed theology harmed every woman in the pews. And I know I'm not alone in this; far too many pastors, other male leaders, and Christian men in general have been abusive to women in the Christian community without ever fully recognizing or owning it.

During the years I was a pastor, I only saw the issues of sexism and abuse in the church from a place of maleness and from a position of power. In other words, I did not see the issue clearly at all and was part of the problem. And because of my privileged position, I did not see the whole story of women's experience in the church for decades.

Now, twenty years later and thirteen years sober from pornography abuse, I see the issue much more clearly. And I want to help other men avoid the pitfalls, learn to relate differently, begin to enact changes to systemic problems in our churches, and treat women as God-breathed equals.

Yes, Pornography Is Abuse

From about age thirteen to my midtwenties, I was a regular consumer of pornography, though I sometimes had long periods of sobriety. Pornography taught me to devour women rather than honor them. It filled in the gap of silence about all things sexual that my parents and church did not teach. The lessons I learned from porn nearly killed me and my future ability to have healthy relationships. Thankfully, I began to heal my past wounds and outgrow my use of porn to numb my emotional pain. I have now been sober longer than I was addicted. But it took years to change my pornographic mindset and style of relating to the world. I had to relearn how to engage beauty and how to face difficult emotions rather than pacify them. I had to heal the wounded little boy who was still living inside of me, looking to be soothed and loved. This work was difficult, but the liberation I have today is well worth it. Many women in my study also brought up pornography and the way it was engaged (or not) in their church. The overall belief they reported witnessing was a collective apathy and an acceptance that the issue is common to all men. I argue that it is rather an issue based on a deep-seated hatred of the feminine.

Though pornography has existed for centuries, it has never existed quite like it does today: any type of fantasy you can imagine, however dark it may be—it is available to you 24/7. In your pocket. Instantly. A generation of men's minds, including the men in our churches, have been hijacked by pornography. These men have developed a pornographic mindset and pornographic style of relating, and sadly, this is playing out in our churches and in how church-attending men engage with women. Internet pornography has set the stage for men to live out their sexual appetites and fantasies in real life by creating an unconscious misogyny and further strengthening the culture of systemic patriarchy in our churches.

In 2014, the Barna Group launched a nationwide study on pornography and titled its resulting report "The Porn Phenomenon." They reported, "Most pastors (57%) and youth pastors (64%) admit they have struggled with porn, either currently or in the past."[1] Yes, even our most sacred places, our churches, have become influenced by pornography. And the problem is not limited to men, though they suffer from its influence more. Overall, 56 percent of women under age twenty-five seek out pornographic materials; 81 percent of teen and young adult men seek it out.[2]

What I have seen in my own life and in the lives of my clients is that the large amount of consumption of porn by men specifically has led to a baseline of objectifying women. A longing to conquer, possess, and devour beauty rather than to honor it is considered acceptable, even "natural." This objectification only strengthens the common posture in our society and in our churches of unconscious misogyny toward women. We are loathe to admit how greatly and broadly this porn mindset impacts men in our churches and how much it contributes to the trauma and abuse of so many women. But if we want to create safe churches, we can no longer afford to look away.

Porn Abuse Amplifies Misogyny in Our Culture

Misogyny is defined as "the dislike of, contempt for, or ingrained prejudice against women."[3] Writer Pamela Paul, in "From Pornography to Porno to Porn: How Porn Became the Norm," states,

> Countless men have described to me how, while using pornography, they have lost the ability to relate to or be close to women. . . . They found the way they looked at women in real life warping to the pornographic fantasies they consumed on screen. Their daily interactions with women became pornified. Their relationships soured. They had trouble relating to women as individual human beings.[4]

I and hundreds of men I have worked with have had to face the truth of this in our lives as we walked the difficult journey of healing from pornography use. Objectifying women online impacts how we treat women in our real-life relationships. It can be subtle. But the pornography gets into our brains, and we unconsciously live it out. I call this dynamic "the pornographic style of relating." When porn becomes our main mentor for our sexuality, it distorts our way of relating to the world, specifically to women. We relate to women the way we relate to porn, which taught us how to be sexual.

Many men develop a love-hate relationship with women as a result of the warping of their minds through pornography. We believe somewhere in our being that women are there to serve men and bring us pleasure. When women don't meet our needs, many men can become aggressive, entitled, and misogynistic.

Now imagine the impact this has on women when they attend a church. For example, consider a pastor who is secretly involved with using pornography and holds deep shame because of his double life and lack of authenticity. He'll be predisposed to two extreme responses. On the one hand, he may inappropriately seduce the women he is around, making them feel adored and special and incredibly cared for and loved. Though this "care" and "niceness" can come across as respect, it is anything but. These women are just props/dolls to be played with and used for his own selfish fulfillment, then recycled to affirm his own insecurities and act as anesthesia for his unhealed core wounds. On the other hand, he may engage in the complete opposite way by leaving the door open during one-on-one meetings with women, convincing himself that his actions are above reproach, being overly guarded and closed off, shaming women in his congregation for wearing "inappropriate" clothing, becoming extremely legalistic, or having so much contempt and hatred for women that it bleeds into every interaction. This man won't take feedback or allow women's words to affect him. His unconscious thought is, *Women are a part of my shame; I hate my shame, so I hate women.*

Porn Abuse Deepens Systemic Patriarchy's Grip on Culture

A 2001 Ryan J. Burns study, "Male Internet Pornography Consumers and Their Attitudes toward Men and Women," looked at heterosexual men who used pornography. The study found that the more pornography a man consumed, the more likely he was to describe women in sexualized and stereotypically feminine ways, to approve of women in traditionally female occupations, and to value women who are more submissive and subordinate to men.[5] These effects of pornography use further prop up an already deeply embedded system of patriarchy.

Remember, *patriarchy* is "a system of society or government in which men hold the power and women are largely excluded from it."[6] Once misogyny is deeply entrenched into the male psyche, the natural progression is patriarchy. With the unconscious posture that "women are less than," men take their so-called rightful places of power with women serving as their stepladder, making sure men retain that power. This is made possible in part by women's own internalized misogyny and sexism. "Internalized sexism is defined as the involuntary belief by girls and women that the lies, stereotypes and myths about girls and women that are delivered to everyone in a sexist society are true."[7] This is just as true in the church as outside it, and, in some cases, even truer. That narrative needs to change.

A Challenge to Men

One of the biggest ways men can begin to change the current trend of sexism and abuse in the church is by taking responsibility for their past, current, and future failures. I know this is a big ask, yet it can be done. It is a difficult and humbling journey to take, and many men are frankly too cowardly to attempt it.

And yet, daily, men on this journey come into my office, and it is gloriously beautiful and wildly gutsy. Men owning their darkness. Men weeping over the harm they have perpetrated against women and over their past leadership failures. Men stepping into the fullness of their power and healthy anger against their own abusers in their painful stories, no longer allowing their unaddressed pain to continue to poison their interactions with others.

Good men are out there, and I am honored to have a front row seat to their courage. We can do this work; we created this problem, and we can help change it. Following are a few small, practical steps all men can take and integrate into their lives to help create safe churches and start their journey of becoming advocates for women.

1. Honor and Do Not Devour Women

"Hey, dude, look at her _____!" Fill in the blank with all the idiotic, asinine things you have heard or even said in the past. This anatomizing women to fit our pornographic fantasies is a posture of devouring, not honoring. It is a toxic male norm and must stop. She is a whole person, a wonderfully complex being created in God's image, and for you to part her out like a used car is to curse the very face of God. Ask yourself, *Why do I dissect her so flippantly? What need am I trying to fill by acting like this?*

What if you started to become more aware of your actions and how you mentally engage with women? What if you worked to challenge objectifying thoughts with the truth that women are whole persons? We cannot change the damaging norm of sexism and abuse if we continue to perpetuate it.

2. Stop Denying Your Failures

You will not cease to exist if you admit you are wrong or that you have been part of the problem. If you can own how you have failed women in the past and/or continue to do so now, this is the first step toward moving beyond sexualization and its firstborn son, patriarchy. Author, artist, and teacher Tiziana DellaRovere says,

> Men must take responsibility to change the violent and destructive aspects of patriarchy side by side with women. Whether you have violated women or not, you must commit yourself to transforming the misguided, patriarchal values and attitudes that you have internalized if you want a life founded on love and a society based on equality, compassion and creative abundance.[8]

This owning your failures must lead to humility, not humiliation. Beating yourself up or going to toxic shame is not the answer to becoming an advocate for women. Humbly owning how you have been a part of the problem and actively changing your behavior will help create safety in our churches.

3. Quit Being a Bystander to Sexism

I am still trying to be more courageous when it comes to standing up to sexism. A few years ago at my tennis club, my coach commented on a woman's body and made an inappropriate joke. I froze. I couldn't believe what I was hearing. I didn't laugh and tried to change the subject. I wish I had been braver in that moment. I eventually went to the director and reported the incident, but I could have been bolder when it mattered most. The "boys' club" is a powerful force that keeps us silent and keeps the culture of sexualization and abuse firmly intact. We must courageously speak up when we hear and see other men objectify women—not only for women's benefit but for our own as well. Men are not animals. We, too, are created in God's image and are called to act accordingly. Toppling this narrative is men's responsibility to bear since we are the ones who continue to uphold it.

4. Listen to Women

Men must listen to women. Stop being condescending or patronizing and change your posture toward women. You are possibly unaware of the daily hell that women suffer, simply because you are not a safe person for them to confide in. Humble yourself. Start listening to their pain without answers, without defensiveness, and without trying to fix anything. Women are not broken, they just need to be heard, their pain understood. As men, we can be powerful advocates of women rather than abusers who spinelessly endorse their oppression.

An Invitation to Men

I truly believe in men.
I believe in our goodness.
I believe in our ability to self-reflect,
To break down and let go,
To be humble,

To change,

To heal.

Men, this is your invitation to join me in this conquest against sexism and abuse. It will be fierce, not in the bloody, cinematic way we may think but in a slow, courageous, non-flashy way. We will be doing our own hard, therapeutic work, facing our shadows, and telling the truth—first to ourselves and then to those around us. As we walk in deep integrity and courage, we honor God, which is to honor all who bear God's image.

TEN

Healing for All

The healing path must pass through the desert or else our healing will be the product of our own will and wisdom. It is in the silence of the desert that we hear our dependence on noise. It is in the poverty of the desert that we see clearly our attachments to the trinkets and baubles we cling to for security and pleasure. The desert shatters the soul's arrogance and leaves body and soul crying out in thirst and hunger. In the desert, we trust God or we die.

Dr. Dan Allender, *The Healing Path*

Whether you are a woman or a man, an important part of healing your trauma of sexism and abuse within the church is writing your church story. Sexism and abuse hurt us all, and every one of us needs healing. However, we cannot heal what we don't first adequately acknowledge or name. In all my workshops, I have each participant write out the stories of pain and heartache that shaped them. Normally, these stories still have power or still impact how they do relationships today. We all have stories that have caused us shame or prompted us to make a vow that forever informed how we relate.

But before I have the participants share their stories with the group, I first share mine. Now, I do these retreats monthly and have been leading them for nearly fifteen years, so I share my story often. But I want to lead with my own blood, my own vulnerability, so when I feel the story of my own pain is in danger of becoming rehearsed or no longer moves me, I write another story from my life. If I want my clients to face their own pain and go to their own emotional edge, then to lead with integrity, I must do the same each time. I cannot expect them to go to places emotionally that I am unwilling to go myself. And nearly each time I force myself to face my pain and share transparently, it inspires the group to do the same. I have experienced some of the most holy and healing moments of my life in sharing stories with others.

In the 1980s, psychologist James W. Pennebaker studied the impact of expressive writing. He divided participants into two groups and had the first group write emotively about their traumas, expressing their deepest feelings about their particular story (i.e., emotionally present). He had the other group write their trauma stories as well but as objectively and factually as possible (i.e., emotionally distant). Both groups wrote for fifteen minutes a day over four consecutive days.[1]

The first group found that though the writing was upsetting, it was meaningful, valuable, and helpful in many areas of their lives. This type of expressive soul writing strengthens the immune system, lessens anxiety and depression, and improves overall health.[2] The second group did not benefit in these life-changing ways. Emotionally present storytelling must be done for all areas of life impacted by trauma, including church trauma.

Writing Your Story

Before you begin writing your story, it is important to have safeguards in place. Do you have a good therapist to help hold the grief? Do you have a trusted friend or mentor? Are you in a place where it is safe to mourn without repercussions? You have to create a safe place so you can feel all the feelings that need to be faced.

What are the particulars of your story? Write the scene in descriptive detail. What did you see? Be expressive and specific, even if you can't remember exactly. Go with your feelings, even if you feel you may be making something up. It's more impressionistic artwork than realism, more about what you are feeling than what you are thinking. What were the sounds? Describe what you heard. Even if it was silence, describe how that silence made you feel.

What did your body feel? This is important because the body holds trauma in a unique way. So if you are describing a time when a deacon looked at you inappropriately or a pastor you trusted texted you a sexual joke that made you feel uncomfortable, journal about your physical feelings. Name them: gross, used, special, aroused. There are no bad answers—it's just data to help your body process very confusing stories of trauma. Try to not judge yourself or your body's reaction.

What did the person say or not say? Words can be a powerful part of the grooming process and can become embedded within us. They need to be extracted. In eighth grade, my male science teacher called me a "slimy slug who leaves his little trail everywhere he goes." Why would I still remember that silly curse some thirty years later? I was an orphaned boy desperately looking for father figures everywhere in my life, so older men's words to me carried a lot of weight, and his words marked me deeply.

If I were writing about that story, I would need to find a way to reclaim those words—confront that teacher with the truth in my imagination—with power that I did not have back then but could process now. I must grieve not only what happened but what didn't happen. (In other words, I can grieve the fact that I felt alone and had no one to talk to or help me process the pain.)

Our harmful church stories are no different from any other stories, and for us to be liberated in our relationship with God, we must enter grief and reclaim the stories of crucifixion so we can taste the goodness of resurrection.

Grief Work

After you have honored your story by being specific about it, it is time to truly feel its depths. This is why it's important to bring as much detail as possible to writing your trauma narrative; you are attempting to reawaken your body. Our bodies store our trauma, and we must enter our bodies to come back into full emotional and spiritual alignment. Grieving all that was decimated is part of entering your body. Grief excavates the soul in the preparative work of God. As the apostle Paul reminds us in Romans 8:17: "If indeed we suffer with him [Christ] . . . we may also be glorified with him." There is no glory without the heartache. To be Christ followers means we will face grief, heartache, and trauma, but we can also experience glory and resurrection on the other side.

By going through this doorway and making peace with suffering, we will no longer be gripped by our church trauma stories. They will no longer guide us from the shadows. When we grieve our great losses—of innocence, trust, community, relationships, and, yes, even faith—we can truly heal and begin to live in abundance once again.

What does grieving look like? Well, it looks like a lot of different things. I lost my dear sister-in-law a few years ago to cancer. It happened too quickly—during Christmas, we celebrated her remission, played games, laughed, and told stories of the future. In March, her cancer returned. A few weeks later, in April, I held her hand in the hospital and stood next to my brother as he made the impossible decision to take her off life support. It felt cruelly quick. I was not ready to say goodbye, to never talk with her again. It felt like a sudden car accident; the whiplash lasted for years. At her funeral service, the pastor told us to wipe our tears away since she was now in heaven. I cried harder, not because she was in heaven but because she was no longer with us.

I still regularly feel the weight of her absence, miss her laughter at my inappropriate jokes, and miss the beauty of her heart and voice. I want to hear her wheeze when she laughed. We only saw each other once or twice a year, as we lived across the country, so my heart feels ready to reunite this Christmas; my mind knows I will not. I must invite grief to baptize me, for the hope of liberation is in the waters of the pain.

This example of grief at my sister-in-law's death seems like an easy one. Of course, you would grieve someone's death, but grief is connected to the level of love. In other words, if you love much, then you must grieve much. I loved my sister-in-law, so I must feel the weight of her loss and mourn her absence. Did you love your church? Did you love the people? Your friends? The pastor, the staff? The one kind old man who greeted you at the door every Sunday? If love was present, then grief must be also. Trauma and abuse cause devastating loss and can feel much like the death of a close family member or friend.

Healing is never a straight line but rather an awkward, wonky, lopsided maze where, most of the time, we don't know which direction is up. But we stumble forward, trying our best to live in grief, grace, and truth, knowing that following the gospel is accompanying Christ into both death and new life.

You are never too far gone and it is never too late to experience liberation from victimization. This is not the last chapter of your story but very much the beginning of using your story of heartache not only for your own freedom but also for the freedom of others who have experienced the terror that you know so well.

Healing for Male Pastors and Leaders

Men, what is the work of a male leader or pastor in healing? In your church, healing starts with you. In other words, if you are not healthy, your leadership will not be healthy, and your congregation will feel the weight of mending *your* burden. You cannot take people further than you have gone yourself.

Your spiritual health is directly connected to your emotional health. I don't know anyone who is spiritually healthy who isn't also emotionally healthy. That is because God is integrated within us, and we cannot be separated within ourselves. We are fully whole, and our emotional, spiritual, and sexual selves are interwoven and informed by one another. So our healing cannot be one-dimensional but must fully include all that makes us human.

If you want to help change the damaging trend of mistreating women, then you must first look deeply inward. Abuse advocate Rachel Peters wrote the following on my Facebook page, and I share this with her permission:

> I don't think a church can be safe for women until men do the hard work of self-reflection into their own lives [and] they recognize their faulty beliefs about women and come face-to-face with their own demons. They must get to a place of emotional vulnerability and refuse to engage in hierarchical behavior that hides their shortcomings and excuses other men from being held accountable for their behaviors. When these things happen, a change in how a church functions in its leadership and its views on women can now be addressed. But if we only try to add a different set of beliefs to a faulty structure it will never succeed. Men must do the hard work.[3]

Men who lead, you must take the long, hard journey of self-reflection and do the hard work that many men don't have the courage to do. Ask yourself the tough questions. What is your own story with the feminine, with your mother, and with your sexuality? What is your history with abuse, objectification, and pornography use? How might these experiences inform your theology and views, your posture toward women, and your leadership style?

These territories must be explored, examined, grieved, and cleaned out for you to lead both women and men from a place of health. This is called *story work*, a narrative-based approach to therapy in which you engage your story—the dynamics of your family of origin and your past traumas that have shaped how you relate with others and with the world. Story work is vital to your ability to lead from a healthy, integrated, centered place. (If you want to learn more about your story, see Dr. Dan Allender's book *To Be Told* and the work of the Allender Center for further growth.)

It will hurt, but remember that crucifixion comes before resurrection. The journey inward creates a courageously broken and humble leader who is safe and ready to lead.

This challenge may well overwhelm you. Pastors have so much on their plates. Managing people is like herding feral cats, and it's one of the loneliest jobs out there. And yet, though we have discussed many failures of leaders and pastors, they are needed now more than ever. But we need courageously broken and humble leaders, leaders who lead differently than in times past.

The courageously broken leader is free from pretense. Authenticity and integrity guide their behavior and how they operate. They know how to differentiate between their own worth as a person and the so-called success or failure of their church. They know their own story and how their story impacts their life. They have become intimate with their core wounds and make sure those wounds don't ruin their life behind the scenes. Since they know who and why they are, they can lead others more wholeheartedly and have more compassion for those who have been harmed by the very institution they represent.

To understand this idea of the courageously broken and humble leader, let's look at Luke 18:9–14:

[Jesus] also told this parable to some who trusted in themselves that they were righteous and looked down on everyone else: "Two men went up to the temple to pray, one a Pharisee and the other a tax collector. The Pharisee was standing and praying like this about himself: 'God, I thank you that I'm not like other people—greedy, unrighteous, adulterers, or even like this tax collector. I fast twice a week; I give a tenth of everything I get.'

"But the tax collector, standing far off, would not even raise his eyes to heaven but kept striking his chest and saying, 'God, have mercy on me, a sinner!' I tell you, this one went down to his house justified rather than the other, because everyone who exalts himself will be humbled, but the one who humbles himself will be exalted."

The story Jesus shares in this passage gives us a picture of a courageously broken and humble individual whom pastors can model themselves after. The self-sufficient, proud man was all about image and looking good for the crowd. Does that sound like any of the churches you've been part of? What if leading well isn't about appearing successful but about keeping a humble and contrite heart toward God and those who bear his image?

In my therapeutic practice, I hear from folks who have proud delusions and abusers who are so blinded by self-importance they cannot clearly see their sin. They will trample anyone who stands in their way, many times using God to justify their contempt, masking it as piety. It is heartbreaking, and many people who get in their way are wounded.

One example is the well-documented abuse by former Seattle pastor Mark Driscoll. So many good-hearted folks I know tried to intervene by talking directly to Mark and reflecting on their experience of him to him, yet his stubborn commitment to his own self-importance blinded him to the wounds he was inflicting. This left therapists in the Seattle area, including me, trying to mend the broken lives he left behind.

But part of him knew what he was doing, as he said, "There is a pile of dead bodies behind the Mars Hill [Church] bus, [laughter], and by God's grace, it'll be a mountain by the time we're done.

You either get on the bus, or you get run over by the bus. Those are the options. But the bus ain't going to stop!"[4] What is the posture of this comment? Do we hear humility, kindness, and brokenness for all the shattered lives he left in his wake? No. What I hear is arrogance and self-righteousness without compassion or a heart for the broken.

Such stories are discouraging, but they aren't the only stories. I counsel men every week who are ready and willing to address their dark, shameful places within and come to peace with their story. These men are bold and brave, ready to repent and change their lives. Pastors are no different from other men, but many have to push through an environment that keeps them isolated and hinders them from emotional growth.

Change is possible for you too, but it will hurt. Repentance always comes with pain; contrition without struggle cannot be trusted. Cheap repentance is now commonplace, taking the form of manipulation, as we've all seen. If someone is authentically broken, however, it will be evidenced by gut-wrenching life change. Which kind of man do you want to be?

I have been in both of these positions at different times. It is much more comfortable to be the self-sufficient man than the broken one, but when I have courageously entered my brokenness, I've experienced God more fully and have been made a better man. I am convinced now more than ever that Jesus knew what he was talking about when he said, "Everyone who exalts himself will be humbled, but the one who humbles himself will be exalted" (v. 14).

ELEVEN

Steps toward Creating a Safe Church

Yes, the church is part of the good news of Jesus. And the church proclaims the good news of Jesus. But when men and women have only seen churches formed by unhealthy power, celebrity, competitiveness, secrecy, and self-protection, our corporate ecclesial life belies the truth of the gospel. The church can only witness to the truth of Jesus by seeking justice, serving with humility, operating transparently, and confessing and lamenting failures.

Scot McKnight, *A Church Called Tov*

There is a huge problem in the church that must be addressed head-on. But what can any of us do to change it? Much of the time, I feel so powerless to make a difference. I am a white man with a doctorate. I used to be a pastor. I am a therapist with influence in the church. Even so, I don't know if I can change the system. I can only imagine how disheartening the idea of affecting change must be for others in less privileged positions. What if you are a woman who has been silenced or dismissed in the past? What if you don't have the right contacts or a formal degree? What if you feel like people don't listen to you or value your voice? Is there anything you can do?

Yes.

There are practical steps we can all take in our congregations to lessen the harm and create safer and more equal places of worship. Let's look at a few of them that can help launch us on the journey.

For Women: Changing Your Church as a Member

I don't purport to be an expert on what women can or should do. Women are experts on the lives of women. I am happy, however, to pass on some wisdom I've received from women in my study, my interviews, and beyond.

Start the Conversation

Whether it's with the help of this book, other resources, or a book study with a few friends, it's time to at least start the conversation with your community. Maybe you even feel safe enough to go to your pastor and share what you have been learning. Whatever you feel like you must do, begin to talk and use your voice. If your voice is not heard and not respected (at the very least), maybe it's time to look for a new community where you will be valued and honored. Remember, being heard is not the same as being agreed with, but it does mean being honored as an image bearer of God.

Use Trusted, Researched, Up-to-Date Resources for Study and Discussion

Many resources used to teach in our church communities today are outdated and downright dangerous. Author Sheila Gregoire and her team at Bare Marriage have done a great job of exposing these teachings and showing why they are harming the Christian community rather than uplifting it. Their research has identified certain common teachings in the church about marriage, sex, and gender roles that actually lead to unsatisfying sex lives and less fulfilling marriages. So please use discernment when seeking out trusted guides. Right now, you can go to BareMarriage.com to test your material and receive its toxic teaching score. Here are some other voices with strong research and a solid history of advocacy that I have come to trust in this space: Sarah McDugal; Jay Stringer; Michael Cusick and his counseling center; Chris Bruno who leads ReStory Counseling; Adam Young and his podcast, *The Place We Find Ourselves*; Dan Allender and the Allender Center; Natalie Hoffman; theologian Peter Enns; and Dr. Gabor Maté.

Find Your People

So many individuals are looking for their people. They have felt disenfranchised, alone, and alienated in their own churches and families. They know something is off in their bodies, and they are looking for language and help to understand what they are feeling without throwing away all of Christianity. This is important. You are not alone in your beliefs that women belong side by side with men, leading the church. You are not anti-Bible because you do not think patriarchy is God's plan for us. When you find your people, that strength and knowledge can help you to go out and use your newfound power and voice. It is a glorious change to witness. It may be difficult because of geography or if you live in a region that is more isolated, but with online groups budding up all over the world, I am confident you can get connected with support no matter where you are located. For example, I know Natalie Hoffman and Sarah McDugal both have strong online communities for women who are going through abuse and looking for like-minded support.

Hold on to Your Power

I am so deeply grieved by how many women attempt to become small, trying their hardest to become less: less attractive, less brilliant, less strong. Kara shared,

I have felt certain men become threatened by my capacity. I have not been allowed to serve on my elder's board because I am a woman. I have been told that I cannot do certain things because of my gender. It has left me feeling that I need to make myself smaller in order to keep the peace in my church settings, and stirring the pot is sinful. Which means that I have felt like parts of my passion and voice have died since being involved in my church.

Kara's story is the story of so many women. I wonder how many of you have been swayed to dim your glory and shun your goodness because of male insecurity. I am sure I could collect an entire library of heartbreaking stories from women around the globe who can relate to these words: "I have compromised my strength because I wanted to be accepted by an insecure man."

Do not shrink so that men won't feel insecure in your presence. That is their work, not yours. Your skill, capability, and capacity are meant to be abundant, and the type of men you want in your life should see that, not want to consume it. If you are a gifted leader, teacher, writer, communicator, organizer, or whatever you find yourself thriving in, it is time for you to step into your power and see what comes as your glory is expanded.

These are a few helpful tips for women to begin to change church culture as members of the body. But what about men who are pastors, elders, or other leaders in the church?

For Men: Changing Your Church as a Leader

We have talked about the importance of pastors and leaders doing their own healing work, knowing they cannot lead others to deep places if they have not first taken their own journey toward inner healing by addressing their own wounded places and taking seriously their own origin stories and early childhood pain. Only after that step is taken comes developing and implementing church policies and safeguards that encourage safety and equality throughout the entire congregation.

But where to begin? The Safe Church Ministry of the Christian Reformed Church shares this example of a policy regarding reporting suspected abuse:

> All ministry leaders/volunteers who have a reasonable suspicion of sexual, physical, or emotional abuse or neglect of a minor or vulnerable adult are responsible to report it within 24 hours to the Child Protective Services/Children's Aid Society 24-hour hotline. . . . If you are uncertain of whether what you heard or saw constitutes evidence of abuse, consult with a member of Model Policy CRC's Safe Church Team.[1]

This is one example of a policy that can help make a church a safer place for people. If this policy had been a part of our study participants' churches, surely some of the victims of sexism and abuse would have been spared.

Other recommended policies churches can implement are regular abuse-prevention training, criminal background checks for staff and volunteers, training to ensure familiarity with the church's policies and reporting procedures, open dialogue sessions, and, finally, increased diversity in leadership positions.

Require Regular Abuse-Prevention Training

Church staff and volunteers should go through regular (annual or semiannual) abuse-prevention training, including training in the proper code of conduct and ethics of leadership, offered by an outside organization with trained professionals.

For example, the organization Godly Response to Abuse in the Christian Environment (GRACE) offers abuse-prevention training to Christian communities. Once leaders complete the training, churches receive a safeguarding certification. GRACE offers training to leaders, adults, and children at age-appropriate levels so congregants are better informed. "The GRACE team is composed of mental health experts, former prosecutors, and pastors who possess a combined experience of over 100 years addressing abuse-related issues."[2]

Boz Tchividjian, the executive director of GRACE, argues that one way Christians can help end systemic abuse in the church is by developing safeguards. However, "the most thorough and well-written policy is powerless unless it becomes part of the very DNA of the church community."[3] This means ensuring members not only have a copy of the policy but also fully understand it. Further, members should be offered ongoing training opportunities held in tandem with church leadership and abuse-prevention experts.

Run Criminal Background Checks

A criminal background check should be required for all staff and volunteers. This simple procedure can be implemented to help safeguard children and women who may be vulnerable to predatory behavior. Now, this is not somehow the be-all and end-all. Just because this step is followed doesn't equate to safety, but it is a baseline, simple step that many churches still do not follow or mandate for their volunteers. If the church you are attending doesn't do this basic step, then they probably will not take the issue of safety seriously.

Schedule Awareness Training of Policies and Reporting Procedures

All staff and volunteers need to have an awareness of proper policies and reporting procedures, which will create a safer church environment. During onboarding, these policies and procedures need to be an integral part of training. The church also needs continued training and reminders of the proper policies and procedures so staff and volunteers do not forget. It is easy to think that these issues simply won't happen in your church, but if you have read this far, you know that no one can remain ignorant. We, as a church, cannot put our heads in the sand and pretend any longer.

Offer Open Dialogue Sessions

Abuse, power dynamics, and sexism should be regularly discussed as a community, with open dialogue, so all congregants are well-informed.[4] When these topics are perceived as taboo, they are less likely to be spoken about and more likely to be hidden. When pastors and other leaders hold transparent conversations about sexism and abuse, it is much easier for any issues or occurrences to be brought to the surface and exposed. This starts from the top—if church leadership does not feel comfortable discussing these difficult topics, the congregation will not either. We cannot expect these conversations to just happen; no one wants to talk about evil in our midst. This may look like holding a biannual meeting for the whole church, during which you discuss basically everything from finances to preventing abuse to any other hot topics. My church of thirteen years called this meeting its "state of the union," and it was an important touch point in helping our community be more transparent and open with any concerns and issues.

Increase Diversity in Leadership Positions

Increasing diversity in church leadership can create more kindness, empathy, and understanding. Having a leadership structure that is balanced and represents a variety of ethnicities, disabilities, socioeconomic statuses, and genders can help illuminate necessary change and amplify the voices of the historically oppressed, creating a safer and more equal church environment. As authors Helen Lee and Michelle Ami Reyes state,

> We believe that God's intent is for all of us to lean into the beautiful differences inherent in the body of Christ and to demonstrate in no uncertain terms that the love of Christ ultimately overcomes all barriers and binds his people—his diverse and multiethnic people—in such perfect unity that "the world will know that [God] sent [him]" (John 17:23).[5]

We are all created in God's image—all of us. That means we can know God more fully and uniquely by being in relationship with people who are different from us. We can learn the mysteries of God through understanding the mystery of our neighbors. God is shown more clearly when we have increased diversity and representation of leadership in our churches, and the church can become not only a safer but a more restorative place for everyone.[6] I love the church and have much hope for its flourishing. But for this to happen, women can't be kept off the team. We all must work together as the body of Christ to bring God's presence to earth. Men in particular can do better at mimicking Jesus's posture toward women, and we can all work to understand Scripture more clearly in the context of culture and create a robust and inclusive theology that doesn't harm people. Pastors, you can do your own healing work to become better and more secure leaders, create diverse leadership teams within your churches, and increase the representation of women during the decision-making process so that you don't inadvertently create more trauma and abuse.

Let's work together to attain these goals in our churches, creating a welcoming culture where all of us, from the greatest to the least, can feel safe. Let's build a better future for our children and their children, ensuring that our churches model the love of Christ to others. After all, isn't that what Jesus would do and what we're called to do as well?

CONCLUSION

Creating a Safe Church

I want to add one final note about what this book is and is not.

What it is: an attempt to take all I've learned in the course of my work, studies, and life to prompt discussion and urge church leaders to take emphatic, empathetic steps toward addressing sexism and abuse and women's safety in Christian communities and to effect real change.

What it is not: an attempt to speak for women on issues about which they are the experts. I am not the expert here—I am merely a scribe, sharing what thousands of women and many trustworthy scholars have taught me. I have a few personal stories littered throughout this book, but I am not a woman; thus I am hindered in fully understanding the issue.

Still, I've learned a great deal along the way. This project has taken me three years to complete and has forever changed me. What has surprised me the most is coming to know the courageous women—the wounded warriors—who shared their stories. They were so appreciative, relieved to finally be heard, and honored, even though I was previously part of the problem they faced. They had spent years being silenced and were so ready to tell their truth and help others who also share in their pain.

This book is not theological mansplaining of women's pain; this is one man (me) trying to use his privilege to amplify marginalized women's voices and bring systemic change to a maledominated institution that has caused countless stories of trauma. May you find it both humbling and inspiring. I hope this book has been as disruptive and transformative for you as it has been for me. Together, you and I can be part of the change and the redemption of God's bride.

ACKNOWLEDGMENTS

So many people helped with the creation of this book, especially my wife, Christy. I'll never be able to thank her enough for all the support she provided in pursuing this dream. Second, this book would not have been possible if it were not for the courageous women who responded to my survey and who were willing to share their lives and their heartaches so others could learn from them. I am forever changed because of their input into this project.

Thank you to Dr. Maureen Manning for being a heroine to me in the beginning of this process. A huge thank-you to Lisa Thompson for your editing skills. The new title of Citation "Queen" is fully yours. To Shari Macdonald Strong, your voice was vital in making this book better and so much stronger and wiser. Robin Turici, your edits made this book readable and something I am proud of. Thank you. To Patnacia Goodman and the rest of the team at Baker Publishing for believing in this material and giving it a shot to impact positive change for the future of the church: I am indebted. Also, huge thanks to my online community: you all are such a voice of encouragement and an anchor in this fight against sexism and abuse.

Thank you all.

NOTES

Introduction

1. My methodology was narrative inquiry, which helped me examine these women's life experiences in the church. Narrative inquiry "records the experiences of an individual or small group, revealing the lived experience or particular perspective of that individual." See "Qualitative Study Design," Deakin University, accessed February 28, 2024, https://deakin.libguides.com/qualitative-study -designs/narrative-inquiry.

2. "Pastor Demographics and Statistics in the US," Zippia, September 9, 2022, https://www.zippia.com/pastor-jobs/demographics/.

3. Tony Porter, "A Call to Men," TED Talk video, 10:57, December 2010, https://www.ted.com/talks/tony_porter_a_call_to_men.

Chapter 1 So, What Exactly Is the Problem?

1. Francesca Donner and Emma Goldberg, "In 25 Years, the Pay Gap Has Shrunk by Just 8 Cents," *New York Times*, March 25, 2021, https://www.nytimes .com/2021/03/24/us/equal-pay-day-explainer.html.

2. Trae Vassallo et al., "Elephant in the Valley," Stanford University, 2016, https://www.elephantinthevalley.com/; Trae Vassallo and Michele Madansky, "Silicon Valley Has a Gender Discrimination Problem—and These Women Can Prove It," *Time*, February 18, 2016, https://time.com/4226297/silicon-valley-gen der-discrimination-data-elephant-in-the-valley/.

3. Vassallo et al., "Elephant in the Valley"; Megan Rose Dickey, "'Elephant in the Valley' Survey Sheds Light on Issues Women Face in Tech," TechCrunch, January 11, 2016, https://techcrunch.com/2016/01/11/elephant-in-the-valley-sur vey-sheds-light-on-issues-women-face-in-tech/.

4. Lyman Stone, "Sex Ratios in the Pews: Is There Really a Deficit of Men in American Churches?," Institute for Family Studies, August 12, 2019, https://ifs

tudies.org/blog/sex-ratios-in-the-pews-is-there-really-a-deficit-of-men-in-amer
ican-churches.

5. Mark Chaves, Joseph Roso, Anna Holleman, and Mary Hawkins, "Congregations in 21st Century America," Duke University, 2021, https://sites.duke
.edu/ncsweb/files/2022/02/NCSIV_Report_Web_FINAL2.pdf.

6. Katelyn Beaty, "The Faith-Work Gap for Professional Women," *Christianity Today*, October 9, 2017, https://www.christianitytoday.com/ct/2017/october-web
-only/faith-work-gap-professional-women-barna.html.

7. *Merriam-Webster Dictionary*, s.v. "sexism," accessed February 28, 2024,
https://www.merriam-webster.com/dictionary/sexism.

8. Peter Glick and Susan T. Fiske, "The Ambivalent Sexism Inventory: Differentiating Hostile and Benevolent Sexism," *Journal of Personality and Social Psychology* 70, no. 3 (1996): 491–512, https://doi.org/10.1037/0022-3514.70.3.491.

9. Jayne Leonard, "6 Types of Sexism, Examples, and Their Impact," *Medical News Today*, February 16, 2023, https://www.medicalnewstoday.com/articles
/types-of-sexism.

10. Elisha Fieldstadt, "Missouri Pastor on Leave after Sexist Sermon Preaching Wives Need to Look Good for Their Husbands," NBC News, March 8, 2021,
https://www.nbcnews.com/news/us-news/missouri-pastor-leave-after-sexist-ser
mon-preaching-wives-need-look-n1259998.

11. Glick and Fiske, "Ambivalent Sexism Inventory."

12. Glick and Fiske, "Ambivalent Sexism Inventory."

13. Leonard, "6 Types of Sexism."

14. Jioni Lewis and Ria Tabacco Mar, "Sexism," Boston University, accessed February 28, 2024, https://www.bu.edu/antiracism-center/files/2022/06/Sexism
.pdf.

15. *Merriam-Webster Dictionary*, s.v. "abuse," accessed February 28, 2024,
https://www.merriam-webster.com/dictionary/abuse.

16. "What Is Emotional Abuse?," National Domestic Violence Hotline, accessed February 28, 2024, https://www.thehotline.org/resources/what-is-emotional
-abuse/.

17. Alita Byrd, "Fighting Abuse in the Faith Community," *Spectrum*, July 23, 2021, https://spectrummagazine.org/interviews/2021/fighting-abuse-faith
-community.

18. Byrd, "Fighting Abuse."

19. Scot McKnight, "What Is 'Spiritual' Abuse? A Working Definition," *Christianity Today*, December 2, 2020, https://www.christianitytoday.com/scot-mc
knight/2020/december/what-is-spiritual-abuse-working-definition.html.

Chapter 2 Why We Must Listen to Women

1. Peter Gay, *Freud: A Life for Our Time* (New York: W. W. Norton & Co., 1989), 247–48.

2. Gay, *Freud*, 246.

3. Judy Gammelgaard, "They Suffer Mainly from Reminiscences," *The Scandinavian Psychoanalytic Review* 15, no. 2 (January 21, 2013): 104–21, https://www
.tandfonline.com/doi/abs/10.1080/01062301.1992.10592277.

4. Gammelgaard, "They Suffer."

5. Judith Herman, *Trauma and Recovery: The Aftermath of Violence—From Domestic Abuse to Political Terror* (2022; repr., New York: Hachette, 1992), 16.

6. Simon J. Frankel, "Freud Revised," *The Harvard Crimson*, March 14, 1984, https://www.thecrimson.com/article/1984/3/14/freud-revised-pbbbooks-which -tell-us/.

7. Melissa Febos, *Body Work: The Radical Power of Personal Narrative* (New York: Catapult, 2022), 14–15.

8. Thomas E. Ford et al., "More Than 'Just a Joke': The Prejudice-Releasing Function of Sexist Humor," *Personality and Social Psychology Bulletin* 34, no. 2 (December 4, 2007): 159, https://doi.org/10.1177/0146167207310022.

9. Ford et al., "More Than 'Just a Joke,'" 159.

10. Travis Hale, "How Do You Eat an Elephant?," *Staking the Plains* (blog), October 6, 2015, https://www.stakingtheplains.com/2015/10/06/how-do-you-eat -an-elephant.

11. Diane Langberg, *Redeeming Power: Understanding Authority and Abuse in the Church* (Grand Rapids: Brazos, 2020), 87, emphasis added.

Chapter 3 The Historical Experience of Women

1. Vimal Patel, "Last Conviction in Salem Witch Trials Is Cleared 329 Years Later," *New York Times*, July 31, 2022, https://www.nytimes.com/2022/07/31/us /elizabeth-johnson-witchcraft-exoneration.html; Jess Blumberg, "A Brief History of the Salem Witch Trials," *Smithsonian Magazine*, October 23, 2007, https:// www.smithsonianmag.com/history/a-brief-history-of-the-salem-witch-trials-175 162489.

2. Blumberg, "A Brief History."

3. Patel, "Last Conviction"; Blumberg, "A Brief History."

4. Loren Cunningham, David Joel Hamilton, and Janice Rogers, *Why Not Women? A Fresh Look at Scripture on Women in Missions, Ministry, and Leadership* (Seattle: YWAM Publishing, 2000), 73.

5. Mary Ann Cline Horowitz, "Aristotle and Woman," *Journal of the History of Biology* 9, no. 2 (1976): 184, https://doi.org/10.1007/bf00209881; Rena Pederson, *The Lost Apostle: Searching for the Truth about Junia* (New York: John Wiley & Sons, 2008), 133.

6. Horowitz, "Aristotle and Woman," 134.

7. Cunningham, Hamilton, and Rogers, *Why Not Women?*

8. A. Hauge, "Feminist Theology as Critique and Renewal of Theology," *Themelios* 17, no. 3 (January 29, 2020), https://www.thegospelcoalition.org /themelios/article/feminist-theology-as-critique-and-renewal-of-theology.

9. Gillian Cloke, *This Female Man of God: Women and Spiritual Power in the Patristic Age, 350–450 AD* (New York: Routledge, 1995).

10. Gerda Lerner, *The Creation of Patriarchy* (Oxford: Oxford University Press, 1986).

11. Dr. Catherine E. McKinley, "Sexism and Misogyny: Unpacking Patriarchy and Its Handmaids," *Psychology Today*, May 5, 2022, https://www.psychology

today.com/us/blog/the-well-woman/202205/sexism-and-misogyny-unpacking-pa
triarchy-and-its-handmaids.

12. Rachel Held Evans, "Is Patriarchy Really God's Dream for the World?," *Rachel Held Evans* (blog), June 8, 2012, https://rachelheldevans.com/blog/patriarchy.

13. Evans, "Is Patriarchy Really God's Dream," emphasis added.

14. Evans, "Is Patriarchy Really God's Dream."

15. Beth Allison Barr, *The Making of Biblical Womanhood: How the Subjugation of Women Became Gospel Truth* (Grand Rapids: Brazos, 2021).

16. Cunningham, Hamilton, and Rogers, *Why Not Women?*, 75; Rosemary Radford Ruether, "Sexism and Misogyny in the Christian Tradition: Liberating Alternatives," *Buddhist-Christian Studies* 34, no. 1 (2014): 83–94, https://doi.org/10.1353/bcs.2014.0020.

17. Ruether, "Sexism and Misogyny," 85.

18. Marie-Dominique Chenu, s.v. "St. Thomas Aquinas," *Encyclopedia Britannica*, accessed March 3, 2023, https://www.britannica.com/biography/Saint-Thomas-Aquinas; Ruether, "Sexism and Misogyny," 86.

19. Becky Castle Miller, "Misinterpreting 'Head' Can Perpetuate Abuse," CBE International, December 5, 2017, https://www.cbeinternational.org/resource/misinterpreting-head-can-perpetuate-abuse/.

20. Meagan Dickerson, "Domestic Violence in Medieval Marriages: The Tragic Story of William and Isabel Newport," *Ancient Origins*, April 24, 2021, https://www.ancient-origins.net/history-ancient-traditions/domestic-violence-0015240.

21. Karin Stetina, "What the Reformation Did and Didn't Do for Women," *The Good Book* (blog), October 31, 2017, https://www.biola.edu/blogs/good-book-blog/2017/what-the-reformation-did-and-didn-t-do-for-women.

22. "Promoting Gender Equality to Prevent Violence against Women," UN Women, accessed March 12, 2024, https://iris.who.int/handle/10665/44098.

23. "Broken Silence: A Call for Churches to Speak Out," Sojourners and IMA World Health, June 2014, https://sojo.net/sites/default/files/Broken%20Silence%20Report.pdf.

24. Vicki Lowik and Annabel Taylor, "Evangelical Churches Believe Men Should Control Women. That Is Why They Breed Domestic Violence," *The Conversation*, December 8, 2019, https://theconversation.com/evangelical-churches-believe-men-should-control-women-thats-why-they-breed-domestic-violence-127437.

25. Lowik and Taylor, "Evangelical Churches."

26. Barr, *Making of Biblical Womanhood*, 83.

27. Craig Keener, "Mutual Submission Frames the Household Codes," *Priscilla Papers* 35, no. 3 (Summer 2021), https://www.cbeinternational.org/resource/mutual-submission-frames-household-codes/.

28. Catherine Kroeger, "The Neglected History of Women in the Early Church," *Christianity Today*, January 1, 1988, https://www.christianitytoday.com/history/issues/issue-17/neglected-history-of-women-in-early-church.html.

29. Kroeger, "Neglected History."

30. Marg Mowczko, "Wealthy Women in the First-Century Roman World and in the Church," *Priscilla Papers* 32, no. 3 (Summer 2018): 3–7, https://www

.cbeinternational.org/resource/article/priscilla-papers-academic-journal/wealthy
-women-first-century-roman-world-and.

31. Jeff Miller, "What Can We Say about Phoebe?," *Priscilla Papers* 25, no. 2
(Spring 2011): 16–21, https://www.cbeinternational.org/resource/article/priscilla
-papers-academic-journal/what-can-we-say-about-phoebe; Mowczko, "Wealthy
Women."

Chapter 4 Jesus's Relationship with Women

1. Yousaf Sadiq, "Jesus' Encounter with a Woman at the Well: A South Asian
Perspective," *Missiology* 46, no. 4 (August 18, 2018): 363–73, https://doi.org/10
.1177/0091829618790102.

2. Ruether, "Sexism and Misogyny."

3. Ruether, "Sexism and Misogyny," 93.

4. Raymond E. Brown, *The Gospel According to John I-XII*, Anchor Yale Bible
Studies, vol. 29 (New Haven, CT: Yale University Press, 1966), 170.

5. Tirzah Meacham, s.v. "Female Purity (Niddah 4:1)," *The Shalvi/Hyman
Encyclopedia of Jewish Women*, accessed March 12, 2024, https://jwa.org/ency
clopedia/article/female-purity-niddah.

6. Sadiq, "Jesus' Encounter," 365.

7. Richard Philips, "Reaching People in Evangelism," Ligonier.org, July 30,
2014, https://www.ligonier.org/learn/articles/reaching-people-evangelism#:~:
text=Rabbi%20Eliezer%20taught%2C%20%22He%20that,of%20ethnic%20
and%20cultural%20hatred.

8. Angela Nevitt Meyer, "The Woman at the Well: The Radical Revelation of
John 4:1–42," Medium, December 8, 2014, https://medium.com/positive-theology
/the-woman-at-the-well-the-radical-revelation-of-john-4-1-42-7aa3470f1b18.

9. Jennifer Garcia Bashaw, "'When Jesus Saw Her . . .': A Hermeneutical Response to #MeToo and #ChurchToo," *Review & Expositor* 117, no. 2 (2020):
288–97, https://doi.org/10.1177/0034637320919135.

10. Matthew Williams, "Shame Removed; Honor Received, Part 3," Biola University, June 11, 2011, https://www.biola.edu/blogs/good-book-blog/2011/shame
-removed-honor-received-part-3.

11. Meyer, "Woman at the Well."

12. Rachel Larsen, "Three Reasons to Rethink the Samaritan Woman in John
4," CBE International, November 30, 2022, https://www.cbeinternational.org/re
source/three-reasons-to-rethink-the-samaritan-woman-john-4/.

13. Meyer, "Woman at the Well."

14. Meyer, "Woman at the Well."

15. Meyer, "Woman at the Well."

16. Rebekah Drumsta, "How Did Jesus Treat Women in the Bible?," Chris-
tianity.com, September 29, 2020, https://www.christianity.com/wiki/jesus-christ
/how-did-jesus-treat-women-in-the-bible.html.

17. Yuri Phanon, "Is She a Sinful Woman or a Forgiven Woman? An Exegesis
of Luke 7:36–50 Part I," *Asian Journal of Pentecostal Studies* 19, no. 1 (2016):
59–71, https://www.aptspress.org/wp-content/uploads/2018/06/16-1_Phanon
_Part_1.pdf.

18. Phanon, "Is She a Sinful Woman," 65.
19. Terri Robertson, "Jesus and the Canaanite Woman (Matthew 15:21-28),"
The Bat Blog, August 18, 2017, https://www.pacificasynod.org/jesus-and-the-ca
naanite-woman-matthew-1521-28/.
20. Robertson, "Jesus and the Canaanite Woman."
21. Andrew Carlson, "Faith, Dog," (sermon), Awake Church, Seattle, WA,
August 14, 2021.
22. Joanne Jamis Cain, "Jesus and His Amazing Relationships with Women,"
Orthodox Christian Network, May 15, 2020, https://myocn.net/jesus-and-his
-amazing-relationships-with-women/.

Chapter 5 Problematic Biblical Texts

1. My definition of proof-texting: cherry-picking biblical passages to fit an
already held belief.
2. Sarah Bessey, *Jesus Feminist: An Invitation to Revisit the Bible's View of
Women* (New York: Howard, 2013), 63.
3. Marg Mowczko, "Partnering Together: Paul's Female Coworkers," *Marg
Mowczko* (blog), May 1, 2019, https://margmowczko.com/paul-romans-16-wom
en-coworkers/.
4. "Strong's G1249—diakonos," Blue Letter Bible, accessed October 11, 2023,
https://www.blueletterbible.org/lexicon/g1249/kjv/tr/0-1/.
5. Scot McNight, *The Blue Parakeet: Rethinking How You Read the Bible*
(Grand Rapids: Zondervan, 2018), 255.
6. Mark Kubo, "On 1 Corinthians 14 & Women's Silence in Church," *The
Junia Project* (blog), July 17, 2014, https://juniaproject.com/on-1-corinthians-14
-womens-silence-in-church/.
7. Marg Mowczko, "1 Corinthians 14:34–35 in a Nutshell," *Marg Mowczko* (blog), October 5, 2014, https://margmowczko.com/1-corinthians-1434-35
-in-a-nutshell/.
8. Mowczko, "1 Corinthians 14:34–35."
9. Frances Hiebert, "Cultural and Ideological Influences on the Role of
Women," *Priscilla Papers* 12, no. 3 (July 31, 1998), https://www.cbeinternational
.org/resource/cultural-and-ideological-influences-role-women/.
10. Bessey, *Jesus Feminist*, 67.
11. Alice Mathews, *Gender Roles and the People of God: Rethinking What We
Were Taught about Men and Women in the Church* (Grand Rapids: Zondervan,
2017); Gail Wallace, "5 Reasons to Stop Using 1 Timothy 2:12 against Women,"
The Junia Project (blog), July 14, 2015, https://juniaproject.com/5-reasons-stop
-using-1-timothy-212-against-women/.
12. Wallace, "5 Reasons."
13. Wallace, "5 Reasons."
14. Kyndall Rae Rothaus, "What Does the Bible Say about Women in Ministry?," *Sojourners*, June 14, 2021, https://sojo.net/articles/what-does-bible-say
-about-women-ministry-pastor-preaching-church.

15. Abbey Bigler-Coyne, "The Maternal Magic of Mitochondria," *Biomedical Beat Blog* (blog), May 6, 2020, https://biobeat.nigms.nih.gov/2020/05/the-maternal -magic-of-mitochondria/.

16. Laurie Hanna, "Study Finds There Are 93 Women in the Bible—but They Speak Just 1.1 Per Cent of the Time," *Daily Mail*, February 5, 2015, https://www .dailymail.co.uk/news/article-2940774/Study-finds-93-women-Bible-speak-just -1-1-cent-time.

17. Hanna, "Study Finds."

18. Julie Zauzmer Weil, "The Bible Was Used to Justify Slavery, Then Africans Made It Their Path to Freedom," *The Washington Post*, April 30, 2019, https:// www.washingtonpost.com/local/the-bible-was-used-to-justify-slavery-then-afri cans-made-it-their-path-to-freedom/2019/04/29/34699e8e-6512-11e9-82ba-fcfeff 232e8f_story.html.

Chapter 6 Problematic Theologies and Teachings

1. Haley Horton, "The Unavoidable Link between Patriarchal Theology and Spiritual Abuse," CBE International, January 13, 2021, https://www.cbeintern ational.org/resource/unavoidable-link-between-patriarchal-theology-and-spirit ual-abuse/.

2. Kevin Giles, *Headship of Men and the Abuse of Women: Are They Related in Any Way?* (Eugene, OR: Wipf and Stock, 2020).

3. Alyssa Roat, "What Are Complementarianism and Egalitarianism? What Is the Difference?," Christianity.com, July 5, 2019, https://www.christianity.com /wiki/christian-terms/what-are-complementarianism-and-egalitarianism-what -s-the-difference.html.

4. Barr, *Making of Biblical Womanhood*, 32.

5. Elaine Storkey, "A Liberating Woman: A Reflection on the Founder of Christians for Biblical Equality," *Christianity Today*, July 12, 2011, https://www .christianitytoday.com/ct/2011/july/liberatingwoman.html.

6. Roat, "What Are Complementarianism and Egalitarianism?"

7. Colleen Warner Colaner, "Exploring the Communication of Evangelical Families: The Association between Evangelical Gender Role Ideology and Family Communication Patterns," *Communication Studies* 60, no. 2 (2009): 97–113, https://doi.org/10.1080/10510970902834833. See also "The Danvers Statement," The Council on Biblical Manhood and Womanhood, accessed March 7, 2024, https://cbmw.org/about/danvers-statement/.

8. Katie Lauve-Moon, *Preacher Woman: A Critical Look at Sexism without Sexists* (Oxford: Oxford University Press, 2021).

9. Thomas Frederick, "An Interpretation of Evangelical Gender Ideology: Implications for a Theology of Gender," *Theology & Sexuality* 16, no. 2 (2010): 183–92, https://doi.org/10.1558/tse.v16i2.183.

10. Frederick, "Interpretation."

11. Frederick, "Interpretation."

12. Dietrich Bonhoeffer, *The Cost of Discipleship* (1937; repr., New York: Touchstone, 1995).

13. Bonhoeffer, *Cost of Discipleship*, 44–45.

14. Marg Mowczko, "The Holy Spirit and Equality in the Book of Acts," *Marg Mowczko* (blog), August 28, 2012, https://margmowczko.com/the-holy-spi rit-and-equality/.
15. Marg Mowczko, "The Problem with Modesty and the Problem of Lust," *Marg Mowczko* (blog), December 4, 2015, https://margmowczko.com/the-prob lem-with-modesty-and-the-problem-of-lust/.
16. Mowczko, "Problem with Modesty."
17. Gretchen Baskerville, *The Life-Saving Divorce: Hope for People Leaving Destructive Relationships* (Torrance, CA: Life-Saving Press, 2020), 8.
18. John Pavlovitz, "The Kind of Christian I Refuse to Be," *John Pavlovitz* (blog), October 21, 2016, https://johnpavlovitz.com/2016/10/21/the-kind-of-chris tian-i-refuse-to-be/.
19. John Piper, "God Is Not Male," Desiring God, March 10, 2014, https://www.desiringgod.org/interviews/god-is-not-male.
20. Marg Mowczko, "Is God Male or Masculine?," *Marg Mowczko* (blog), June 22, 2011, https://margmowczko.com/is-god-male-or-masculine/.
21. "Female Images of God in the Bible," Women's Ordination Conference, accessed October 10, 2023, https://www.womensordination.org/resources-old /female-images-of-god-in-the-bible/.

Chapter 7 Understanding Trauma and Abuse

1. "William Tecumseh Sherman," PBS American Experience, accessed October 11, 2023, https://www.pbs.org/wgbh/americanexperience/features/grant -sherman/.
2. Elaine K. Howley, "Statistics on PTSD in Veterans," *U.S. News & World Report*, June 28, 2019, https://health.usnews.com/conditions/mental-health/ptsd /articles/ptsd-veterans-statistics.
3. "Violence against Women," World Health Organization, March 9, 2021, https://www.who.int/news-room/fact-sheets/detail/violence-against-women.
4. "Violence against Women."
5. Jay Shetty, "Gabor Maté and Jay Shetty on Understanding Trauma," *Jay Shetty* (blog), March 10, 2023, https://jayshetty.me/blog/gabor-mate-and-jay-she tty-on-understanding-trauma/.
6. Bessel van der Kolk, *The Body Keeps the Score: Brain, Mind, and Body in the Healing of Trauma* (New York: Penguin, 2015), 21.
7. Peter Enns, *The Bible Tells Me So: Why Defending Scripture Has Made Us Unable to Read It* (New York: Harper One, 2015), 4.
8. Aya Hibben, "Hibben: Recognize Your Own Internalized Misogyny," *Daily Utah Chronicle*, April 23, 2022, https://dailyutahchronicle.com/2022/04/23/hibben -internalized-misogyny/.
9. Hibben, "Hibben: Recognize."
10. Hibben, "Hibben: Recognize."
11. "False Reporting," The National Sexual Violence Resource Center, accessed October 10, 2023, https://www.nsvrc.org/sites/default/files/2012-03/Publ ications_NSVRC_Overview_False-Reporting.pdf.

12. Facts within this letter can be found at North Coast Rape Crisis Team, "Supporting Survivors: Sexualized Violence Statistics," Cal Poly Humboldt, accessed October 10, 2023, https://supportingsurvivors.humboldt.edu/statistics; the author's letter has been edited for space.

Chapter 8 The Church's Present-Day Engagement with Women

1. Barna Group, "Five Factors Changing Women's Relationship with Churches," Barna, June 15, 2015, https://www.barna.com/research/five-factors-changing-womens-relationship-with-churches/.

2. Campbell Leaper and Cristia Spears Brown, "Sexism in Schools: The Role of Gender in Educational Contexts and Outcomes," *Advances in Child Development and Behavior* 47 (2014): 189–223; https://doi.org/10.1016/bs.acdb.2014.04.001.

3. Karoline M. Lewis, "The Truth about Sexism in the Church," *Christianity Today*, June 20, 2016, https://www.christianitytoday.com/women-leaders/2016/june/truth-about-sexism-in-church.html.

4. Byrd, "Fighting Abuse."

5. Byrd, "Fighting Abuse."

6. Byrd, "Fighting Abuse."

7. Matt Zwolinski, "Exploitation and Consent," in *The Routledge Handbook of the Ethics of Consent*, ed. Peter Schaber and Andreas Müller (New York: Routledge, 2018), 153–63.

8. Susan Raine and Stephen A. Kent, "The Grooming of Children for Sexual Abuse in Religious Settings: Unique Characteristics and Select Case Studies," *Aggression and Violent Behavior* 48 (2019): 180–89, https://doi.org/10.1016/j.avb.2019.08.017.

9. Samantha Craven, Sarah Brown, and Elizabeth Gilchrist, "Sexual Grooming of Children: Review of Literature and Theoretical Considerations," *Journal of Sexual Aggression* 12, no. 3 (2006): 287–99, https://doi.org/10.1080/13552600601069414.

10. Anna Salter, *Predators: Pedophiles, Rapists, and Other Sex Offenders* (New York: Basic Books, 2004), 29.

11. Yael Danieli, "Fundamentals of (Re)traumatized Populations," in *Creating Spiritual and Psychological Resilience: Integrating Care in Disaster Relief Work*, ed. Grant H. Brenner, Daniel H. Bush, and Joshua Moses (New York: Routledge, 2010), 195–210.

12. Pam C. Alexander, "Retraumatization and Revictimization: An Attachment Perspective," in *Retraumatization: Assessment, Treatment, and Prevention*, ed. Melanie P. Duckworth and Victoria M. Follette (New York: Routledge, 2012), 191–220.

13. Michael E. Brown, Linda K. Treviño, and David A. Harrison, "Ethical Leadership: A Social Learning Perspective for Construct Development and Testing," *Organizational Behavior and Human Decision Processes* 97, no. 2 (2005): 117–34, https://doi.org/10.1016/j.obhdp.2005.03.002.

14. Bronwyn Lea, "Sex Scandals and the Evangelical Mind," *Christianity Today*, September 6, 2022, https://www.christianitytoday.com/ct/2022/september-web-only/matt-chandler-scandal-sex-abuse-church-evangelical-mind.html.

15. Vanessa Stricker, "How Can We Respond to Failed Church Leaders? Embrace Discernment," *Christianity Today*, April 1, 2022, https://www.christianitytoday.com/better-samaritan/2022/april/how-can-we-respond-to-failed-church-leaders-embrace-discern.html.

16. Lee Colan, "4 Powerful Leadership Lessons from Jesus," *Inc.*, May 1, 2023, https://www.inc.com/lee-colan/4-powerful-leadership-lessons-from-jesus.html.

17. Peter A. Levine, *In an Unspoken Voice: How the Body Releases Trauma and Restores Goodness* (Berkeley: North Atlantic Books, 2010), xii.

18. Leonard T. Gries, David S. Goh, and Jeanne Cavanaugh, "Factors Associated with Disclosure during Child Sexual Abuse Assessment," *Journal of Child Sexual Abuse* 5, no. 3 (1997): 1–19, https://doi.org/10.1300/J070v05n03_01.

19. Kimberly Firth et al., "Healing, a Concept Analysis," *Global Advances in Integrative Medicine and Health* 4, no. 6 (2015): 44–50, https://doi.org/10.7453/gahmj.2015.056.

20. Diane Langberg, "Sexual Abuse in Christian Organizations," accessed October 11, 2023, https://static1.squarespace.com/static/5b0a335c45776ee022efd309/t/5be936628a922d4a291eb2af/1542010466315.

21. Peter Feuerherd, "Women Clergy and the Stained-Glass Ceiling," *JSTOR Daily*, May 28, 2019, https://daily.jstor.org/women-clergy-and-the-stained-glass-ceiling/.

22. Dan Allender, "Excerpt from *Healing the Wounded Heart*," Allender Center, March 10, 2016, https://theallendercenter.org/2016/03/healing-wounded-heart-excerpt/.

23. Allender, "Excerpt from *Healing the Wounded Heart*."

24. Allender, "Excerpt from *Healing the Wounded Heart*."

25. Barna Group, "Five Factors."

26. Barna Group, "Five Factors."

27. Rob Dixon, "Raising Up Allies: A Standardized Pathway for Developing Men into Allies to Women," CBE International, July 31, 2020, https://www.cbeinternational.org/resource/raising-allies-standardized-pathway-developing-men-allies-women/.

28. Diane Langberg, "How Should the Church Respond to Abusers?," DianeLangberg.com, January 6, 2020, https://www.dianelangberg.com/2020/01/how-should-the-church-respond-to-abusers/.

29. Trevin Wax, "I Want a Bigger Bible," The Gospel Coalition, August 13, 2015, https://www.thegospelcoalition.org/blogs/trevin-wax/i-want-a-bigger-bible/.

30. Benjamin M. Bonilla Lopez, "Cultivating Ethnically Diverse Leaders: An Exploration of the Need for Ethnic Diversity in Leadership Positions and Its Potential Impact on Mission Work of the Seventh-Day Adventist Church in Guatemala," *Journal of Adventist Mission Studies* 17, no. 1 (2021), art. 3, https://digitalcommons.andrews.edu/cgi/viewcontent.cgi?article=1483&context=jams.

31. Langberg, "Sexual Abuse in Christian Organizations," 9.

32. Anna Brown, "More Than Twice as Many Americans Support Than Oppose the #MeToo Movement," September 29, 2022, Pew Research, https://www.pewresearch.org/social-trends/2022/09/29/more-than-twice-as-many-americans-support-than-oppose-the-metoo-movement/.

33. Brown, "More Than Twice as Many Americans."

Chapter 9 Speaking Man to Man

1. Barna Group, "The Porn Phenomenon," Barna, accessed October 10, 2023, https://www.barna.com/the-porn-phenomenon/.
2. Barna Group, "The Porn Phenomenon."
3. Claire Brader, "Misogyny: a New Hate Crime?," House of Lords Library, November 22, 2021, https://lordslibrary.parliament.uk/misogyny-a-new-hate -crime/.
4. Pamela Paul, "From Pornography to Porno to Porn: How Porn Became the Norm," American Family Association of Pennsylvania, accessed October 10, 2023, https://afaofpa.org/wp-content/uploads/From-Pornography-to-Porno -to-Porn.pdf.
5. Ryan J. Burns, "Male Internet Pornography Consumers and Their Attitudes toward Men and Women" (PhD diss., University of Oklahoma, 2001), https://share ok.org/bitstream/handle/11244/336/3014515.PDF?sequence=1&isAllowed=y.
6. Institutional Diversity, Equity, Advocacy and Leadership, "Terminology," Temple University, accessed October 11, 2023, https://diversity.temple.edu /terminology.
7. "Internalized Sexism / Internalized Misogyny," Cultural Bridges to Justice, accessed October 11, 2023, https://culturalbridgestojustice.org/internalized-sex ism-internalized-misogyny/.
8. Tiziana DellaRovere, "To Men Who Are Sick of Patriarchy: Here's How You Can Stop It," *The Sacred Lovers Within* (blog), December 4, 2017, https:// thesacredloverswithin.com/men-sick-of-patriarchy-heres-how-you-can-stop-it/.

Chapter 10 Healing for All

1. James W. Pennebaker, "Expressive Writing in Psychological Science," *Perspectives on Psychological Science* 13, no. 2 (2018): 226–29, https://doi.org/10 .1177/1745691617707315.
2. Febos, *Body Work*, 8.
3. Rachel Peters, "Dr. Andrew J. Bauman," Facebook post, September 1, 2021.
4. Mike Cosper, "Episode 1: Who Killed Mars Hill?," *The Rise and Fall of Mars Hill* (podcast), June 21, 2021, https://www.christianitytoday.com/ct/pod casts/rise-and-fall-of-mars-hill/who-killed-mars-hill-church-mark-driscoll-rise -fall.html.

Chapter 11 Steps toward Creating a Safe Church

1. Safe Church Ministry, "Safe Church Model Policy," Christian Reformed Church of North America, June 7, 2022, https://docs.google.com/document /d/1xDwhQ_WB6hfNlPcXZbz1UK5IsOpmPO-m1RS8FIijuCs/edit#.
2. GRACE, "Prevention Tools: Protect Your Faith Community," Safeguarding Initiative, accessed March 12, 2024, https://www.netgrace.org/safeguarding -initiative.

3. Boz Tchividjian, "The One Best Idea for Ending Sexual Harassment," *Washington Post*, December 8, 2017, https://www.washingtonpost.com/blogs/post-partisan/wp/2017/12/08/the-one-best-idea-for-ending-sexual-harassment/#idea11.

4. Safe Church Ministry, "Safe Church Model Policy."

5. Helen Lee and Michelle Ami Reyes, "The Church Was Meant to Enjoy Its Diversity, Not Wish It Away," *Christianity Today*, January 3, 2023, https://www.christianitytoday.com/ct/2023/januaryfebruary/church-was-meant-to-enjoy-its-diversity-not-wish-it-away.html.

6. Lee and Reyes, "The Church Was Meant."

ANDREW J. BAUMAN is the founder and director of the Christian Counseling Center: For Sexual Health & Trauma (CCC) and a licensed mental health counselor. A former pastor, Andrew now works with men and women to bring healing and wholeness to their sexual and spiritual lives. His mission is to use his unique position to elevate women's voices and expose a disease that desperately needs to be removed from the church's body.